Social Theory for a Change

Social Theory for a Change
VITAL ISSUES
IN THE CLASSICS

R. James Sacouman

ACADIA UNIVERSITY

ISBN: 0-7725-2681-8

Canadian Cataloguing in Publication Data available from the National Library of Canada.

Editor: Barbara Tessman
Design: Sonya V. Thursby, Opus House Incorporated
Cover design: Sonya V. Thursby, Opus House Incorporated

Published by:
Irwin Publishing
325 Humber College Blvd.
Toronto, ON
M9W 7C3

Printed and bound in Canada

1 2 3 4 5   02 01 00 99

CONTENTS

Preface vii

ONE
The Enlightenment and a Model of
Social Reasoning 1

TWO
The Enlightenment and Value-
Stances on Humans, Existing
Society, and the Possibility of Radical
Social Change 8

THREE
Elite Engineering I: Auguste Comte's
Positivism and the "Reformist"
Origins of Sociology 15

FOUR
Emancipation Ia: Karl Marx's
Historical Materialism and the
Problem of Human Alienation 24

FIVE
Emancipation Ib: Marx's Political
Economy of Capitalism 33

SIX
Emancipation Ic: Marx's Theory of
Class Struggles and Societal
Transformation 41

CONTENTS

SEVEN
Elite Engineering II: Herbert
Spencer's "Radicalism," Social
Evolutionism, and Constraint
Engineering 48

EIGHT
Elite Engineering III: Emile
Durkheim's Positivist and
Structuralist Corporatism and the
Problem of Socialization 57

NINE
The Middle Road I: Georg
Simmel's Dialectical and Idealist
Structuralism and the Forms of
Social Interaction 66

TEN
The Middle Road IIa: Max Weber's
Historical Idealism and the Types
of Social Action, Power, and
Authority 74

ELEVEN
The Middle Road IIb: Weber's
Theory of Rationalization and the
Prospects for Social Change 83

TWELVE
Elite Engineering IV: Vilfredo
Pareto's Anti-Enlightenment
Irrationalism, Sentiments, and the
Circulation of Elites 91

THIRTEEN
Emancipation II: Vladimir Lenin's
Theory of Uneven Development,
Imperialism, and Socialist
Revolution 99

FOURTEEN
Emancipation III: Rosa
Luxemburg's Dialectical
Materialism and the Critiques of
European Marxisms 109

FIFTEEN
Emancipation IV: Antonio
Gramsci's Critique of Economic
Determinism and Theory of
Hegemony and Intellectuals 118

SIXTEEN
The Middle Road III: Karl
Mannheim's Sociology of
Knowledge, Intellectuals, and the
Third Way 127

SEVENTEEN
The Ongoing Relevance of
Classical Social Theory for a
Change: Vital Issues for Our Times
and Your Theorizing 135

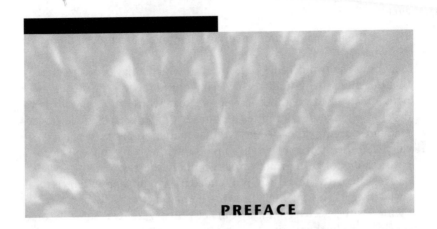

PREFACE

This small book has two related purposes. The first is to introduce undergraduate students and other readers to central issues in classical sociological theory in a way that is understandable, relevant, and motivating. The second is to develop a critical understanding of the continuing importance of key classical insights into the necessity and possibility of social change in our current world. These twin purposes are captured in the title. It suggests that we do social theory more self-consciously for a change, instead of running away from it or pretending that we are not theorizing; and that we understand classical social theory in order to participate more actively in understanding our current situations, individually and collectively, in order to contribute to more, not less, social justice.

For more than twenty years I have taught an undergraduate course in classical sociological theory. Like many others in my situation, I have constantly sought the "perfect" combination of a survey textbook and primary readings. Such a combination would have to provide sufficient detail and rigour. At the same time, it had to convince as many students as possible that grappling critically with the reasoning of "dead, white European males" might actually be, despite the real biases and inadequacies of all these theorists, vitally important.

The available survey texts all seem to presuppose an intellectual motivation in the student readership to rediscover the "fathers" of the discipline, a motivation that goes well beyond mere survival in a required sociology course. In my experience, this presupposed motivation is absent in almost all of even the most committed students. When such motivation is present, survey texts tend to disable committed scholarship by becoming too rapidly locked into endlessly detailing the specific arguments of each great theorist in classical sociology, as if students already knew why the specific arguments of "old farts" mattered.

The legitimate first question of any student of classical social theory is, "So what?"

During the two decades of lectures in which I have tried to answer that question, many students have challenged me to generate an alternative text based on those lectures—a text whose first purpose is to develop a range of committed responses to "So what?" Once undergraduates, or any other people, for that matter, understand why classical social theory can be vitally important, they can and will deepen their reading of both primary and secondary sources.

This alternative text, then, is intended to be both a primer in classical social theory and an invitation to theorize better. It is best supplemented with selected readings from key primary sources and with some delving into further contextual and conceptual details of chosen theorists through essay-writing projects or take-home examinations. I have eschewed copious footnotes in favour of concluding each chapter with a listing of selected key sources and a few questions for further research and debate.

As traditionally conceived, classical social theory was a profoundly European enterprise. The central "problem" within this European tradition was the perceived social crisis associated with the historic change from "premodernity" to "modernity." The central focus within this tradition was on the origins, contemporary structures and processes, and social relevance of this historic social change.

Because this change occurred first within western Europe and then extended outwards, it is not too surprising that the classic theories of the origins, structured processes, and direction of modernity would initially be western European in origin, content, and ideology. Only later, between the two world wars, did it extend into the rest of Europe. While somewhat broadening the array of approaches usually considered, I have done so strictly within this European tradition, with its central problem, central focus, and, as we will see, its usual stress on socially rooted, Enlightened reasoning.

The European tradition of classical social theory, of course, carried more baggage than just its Eurocentrism. At least until the Second World War, it was, for instance, also an entirely white and almost entirely male product of its times, produced almost totally by persons whose class origins were high enough to secure for them an advanced formal education. These additional racial, gender, and class biases have become embedded in the selection of who gets to count as a classical social theorist. As might be expected, they were also often embedded in the theorists and theories themselves. I have maintained their sexist language in all primary material.

Over the last thirty years or so, it has simply not been possible to ignore the major theoretical contributions to social analysis made by some representatives of the world's female and non-white majorities, though the theorizing voices of the impoverished remain, out of necessity, virtually silenced in what gets to count as theory. The main point is that these newer alternative theories never advanced by being ignorant of the European classics. They advanced in critical contestation with them, by knowing them thoroughly and thereby going beyond their limitations. All of us need to do the same.

During the very first class of every course, I inform participants of my Marxist orientation. I ask them to beware of my pushing that orientation upon them and to learn to contest my ideas at every opportunity in order to better develop and test their own approach. I also ask them to beware of merely feeding my orientation back to me in their course work, since I am interested in facilitating and discussing their own theoretical development and not in spoon-feeding pretence. This approach is apparently not very common at our regurgitative universities. Nevertheless, I advocate it as crucial in any social theory course that actually wants to learn about the process of theorizing for a change.

I look forward to hearing comments on the text and its usefulness from professors and students from all possible theoretical perspectives. Among those who have already responded, I am particularly grateful to Bob Russell, Danny Goldstick, Henry Veltmeyer, Debra Richardson, and Doug Meggison for their detailed comments. Publisher Jeff Miller was always helpful and prompt. Editor Barbara Tessman was simply wonderful, both supportive and helpfully critical. I remain certain that social theory for a change can best be developed within a diversity of increasingly well-argued approaches.

Better understanding the necessity and possibility of social change towards social justice has been a central focus in my life for a long time. Growing up in what was called Turkeytown in Winnipeg, I often cursed our relative poverty, my amazingly supportive mother who could never find a way to leave my alcoholic and highly abusive father, and my father who could never quite hold a job. By the time I had fled Turkeytown at eighteen, I was looking for societal alternatives to blaming the victims of personal and collective misery.

This text is dedicated to the memory of my mother and father, Marguerite Eugenie and Robert John Sacouman. Among the living, my deepest thanks and love go to four special women: partner Barbara Moore, sister Lesley, and daughters Natasha and Nicole Sacouman.

The Enlightenment and a
Model of Social Reasoning

ONE

Trying to make sense of the social world around and within us is an everyday event in our lives. Our social interactions continually inform us of how well we make sense of that world. From time to time we make mistakes: sometimes we are told this; sometimes we know this ourselves. In either case, we may choose to do something about it, or we may leave things as they are. If we do choose to act differently, we may or may not actually act. Then, we may even assess the consequences of acting or not acting differently. And so it goes.

We are probably most likely to assess our experiences, insights, choices, and actions in times of crisis, when it seems to be necessary. We are probably most likely to alter our actions when it is understood to be not only necessary but also possible. Necessity *and* possibility are the co-mothers of human, social creativity.

This elementary *epistemology*—or model of how we come to know, choose, and act as human beings—finds its conceptual roots in the *Enlightenment*. It is a central organizing principle in this text that all subsequent social theory responds to, and can be initially understood in terms of, this Enlightenment epistemology.

The Enlightenment was a tremendous intellectual revolution that occurred within a much larger crisis in church, state, and economy. Centred in eighteenth-century western Europe, the Enlightenment both accompanied and helped justify a political-economic-social-cultural transformation of much of Europe, a transformation that has become known, variously, as the industrial, bourgeois, or liberal democratic revolution. While men and women from the peasant and working classes of feudal Europe were massively mobilizing on the streets and in the workplaces and fields, male intellectuals and other male middle-class burghers were setting forth the guiding principles that would sustain, but also strictly limit, the popular demands for "Liberty,

Equality, and Fraternity" promoted most dramatically in the French Revolution.

Basically, within a myriad of contextual variations, the Enlightenment increasingly became a self-conscious and collective reorientation of intellectual life in much of western Europe and in parts of the emerging white-settler colonies. The Enlightenment substituted a profound faith in human *reasoning* for a profound faith in authoritative, traditional, religious, or customary dogma. Human reasoning, it was stressed, could "enlighten" humanity by throwing off the shackles of what was seen to be mystifying superstition. Indeed, human reasoning, Enlightenment theorists argued, could discover reasons for the social acceptance of dogmatic mystifications, in addition to explaining all other aspects of the social and material world.

On the one hand, then, the Enlightenment's faith in human reasoning could "lighten up" the burden of mindless dogma as well as "light" the path forward to human emancipation. On the other hand, Enlightened human reasoning placed a very large burden on the human species and on the individual reasoner to reason well. It clearly privileged humanity over all other species, since none other was seen to be anywhere nearly as reason-able. It also clearly privileged those with the time and resources to fulfil the task or opportunity to reason well—mostly white, upper- or middle-class males. By developing their reason-ability, such people could, by definition, become more completely human than others who could or would not do so.

The Enlightenment itself was firmly rooted in the tradition of Western rationalism that stems from the classical Greek philosophers and was spread throughout the European "world" that was initially forged militarily, politically, and economically by the technological might of the Roman Empire and spiritually (militarily, politically, and economically) by the Roman Catholic Church. As a further specification and reformation of Greco-Roman thought, the Enlightenment, then, is the historical continuation of only one of the available worldviews on the relationship of humans to our "natural," "spiritual," and "social" environment(s).

Many other, very different world-views of the human–environment relationship were developed in other parts of the globe—both in the so-called great, centralized "world empires," such as the Chinese and the Incan, and in the much more numerous and dispersed so-called "primitive" societies. These alternative world-views differed greatly from European rationalism and its technological fixation. The military, political, economic, and spiritual conquest of these peoples and worldviews has been an integral part of the attempted extension of, and integration of the world into, only one acceptable general world-view within only one all-encompassing world political-economic-cultural order that has so typified the modern era from the Enlightenment until the present.

Although the line from Greco-Roman to Enlightenment to current theorizing originated almost entirely in the theorizing of white, European men who could afford the time to reason, its domination as *the* acceptable world-view has become virtually global. Thus, to discard modern social theorizing because of its origins with such men is to trivialize its actual power in the lives of all others, you, perhaps, included. Minimally, all of us need to understand the Enlightenment and its social offspring in some detail in order to confront, critically, its domination in our own lives as well as in the rest of the world. We have to know the dominant world-view as it is expressed in our own thinking in order to evaluate other world-views.

But before we go further, let's look in some depth at the basic Enlightenment epistemology of how we come to know, choose, and act. This epistemology, after all, provided the meta-theoretical, philosophical assumptions for all other political-economic-social-cultural "advances" in "Enlightened" thought.

Enlightenment thinkers generally shared a view that we, as human beings, are distinct from all other species in the known universe because of our advanced capacity for *conscious experience*. No other species, it was said, has the ability, from very early in life, to be as sensate and simultaneously self-sensate. While all living species can experience the external and internal world, at least to some degree, no other species is so aware of the self as experiencing. Conscious and self-conscious experience provided the raw data for reasoning about the world. Our unique ability for conscious and self-conscious experience provided the principal basis for both the necessity and possibility of our species' unique capacity for insight, to reason, to understand and to explain. For many of the Enlightenment thinkers, conscious and self-conscious experience was, by definition, individuated experience, since no other person could ever experience quite the same raw data.

For relatively conservative philosophers, such as the German theorist Immanuel Kant (1724–1804), reasoning about our sensate experience was the crucial emancipatory product of the Enlightenment, the courage to use one's own reasoning as best one can was a moral imperative, and the freedom to do so in public was the principal social-political task to be attained. For the more radically liberal of the French *philosophes*, such as Jean-Jacques Rousseau (1712–78), reasoning could explain both how and why the social world was a system of unnatural enslavement and why and how the system could be transformed through the free consent of individual reasoners. All of the Enlightenment, then, argued that the lack of individual freedom to reason was the crucial social problem in a society dominated by theology

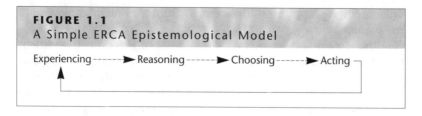

FIGURE 1.1
A Simple ERCA Epistemological Model

Experiencing ------► Reasoning ------► Choosing ------► Acting

and royalty. Where conservative and liberal-radical Enlightenment thinkers tended to split most clearly was with respect to the relation between reasoning, choice, and action.

Liberal-radical political philosophers such as Rousseau tended to reduce reasoning to experimental science and then to argue that human choice and action ought, in a truly enlightened world, best to be directly guided by purely rational-scientific insights. Indeed, Rousseau even developed a "scientific" program of education for the young that would socialize them into a practice of purely rational morality. Liberal-radical political economists such as Adam Smith (1723–90) further reduced individual reasoning, choice, and action to "scientific" supply-and-demand market considerations.

Conservatives such as Kant countered that while science was the purest form of human reasoning, the very relationship between the world and the experiencing knower of that world meant that experimental science could never completely explain the world as such; it could only impose categorical order on the sense experiences of that world. Indeed, rational science could never replace what Kant argued to be the innate capacity of free individuals for moral self-direction.

Whatever the ideological and philosophical differences, we can summarize the main aspects of Enlightenment epistemology in a simple *ERCA model* of human Experiencing, Reasoning, Choosing, and Acting (see Figure 1.1). In a social world of perfect Enlightenment, all individuals could "ERCA" without any limitations to freedom except for the instigating experience itself. Individuals would reason through their experiences, make choices, act upon those choices, and then continuously modify that reasoning, choice, and action on the basis of new experience, which would include that prior experience of ERCAing. This new world would facilitate enlightened human development while introducing an array of new problems rooted in the new freedom to reason and develop.

This world would surely be very different from the interpersonal world of domination and abuse we too regularly exist in. It would be a world of liberty, equality, and solidarity instead of a world that often legitimates personal development by denying others the chance to develop. In our real world, the vast majorities of humanity (by class, ethnicity, gender, age, and so on) are actively disallowed the freedom to develop. How and why does so little liberty, equality, and solidarity exist within the human species? How can, and why should, the species ameliorate or transform this situation? These are the absolutely basic questions that were first posed rationally by Enlightenment theorists.

Before we consider, in the next chapter, a broad mapping of the wide array of social-theoretical responses to these vital Enlightenment concerns, we should not forget that *none* of the Enlightenment thinkers actually considered liberty, equality, and solidarity to be inclusive of all of humanity. They regularly assumed, if not directly argued, that women, non-whites, the impoverished peasantry, and the working classes were simply, if unfortunately, not reason-able. At best, such huge majorities would have to bide their time maturing for another millennium or two under the considerate supervision of their superiors. Such less-than-fully humans might hope to reach maturity and reason-ability by continuing to sweep the floors of, provide the sustenance for, take instruction from, and, in all ways, facilitate the empowerment of the enlightened elite of upper-class, white, European men.

This hole in the whole of Enlightenment inclusiveness becomes abundantly evident if one considers both Rousseau's program for the perfectibility of young men and women through Enlightened education in his *Emile* and the Enlightened rejoinder by Mary Wollstonecraft (1759–97) in her *Vindication of the Rights of Woman*. Rousseau argues that Emile/man must be educated differently from and more rationally than Sophy/woman because of their different natures, women being much more naturally nurturing and practical and much less naturally able to abstract and speculate. Wollstonecraft vigorously criticizes some of Rousseau's biases against women, but consistently argues for the full human rights of only upper- and middle-class women; for Wollstonecraft, lower-class women are doomed to service the Enlightenment of both men *and* an Enlightened minority of relatively elite women.

Enlightenment theory, in summary, may be creatively and critically understood and evaluated on a wide range of fronts. In the spirit of the Enlightenment, its basic epistemology can and should be debated in terms of its applicability in one's own life. Certainly, as we will see, the big issue of whether or not human beings are actually unique and therefore have some degree of creative freedom relative to other species because of their conscious experience and reason-ability has distinguished all later social theory. Even when such theorists have tentatively answered "yes" to relative human uniqueness and creativity, the question of whether pure reason is sufficient for determining choices and actions (*scientism*), or whether human beings are, because of conscious experience, both rational and moral, choice-making actors (*humanism*), continues to divide later classical and contemporary theorizing.

For my own part, I would argue that much insight can be gained by taking the basic epistemology and associated principles of liberty, equality, and solidarity seriously. If we were to do so, then it might become increasingly apparent that these vital principles were sacrificed by Enlightenment thinkers themselves, in the same way that they were sacrificed by the emerging capitalist world system of political-economic-social-cultural organization. The stated concept of liberation of all humanity from oppression was replaced by liberty for some on the backs of many. Equality for all was reduced to equal opportunity to be unequal, or was simply denied. Solidarity with all, a concept that had already been reduced to fraternity, was further reduced to solidarity among one's own immediate interest groupings in competition with, and to the lasting detriment of, all others.

6

Key Sources

Geoffrey Hawthorn's *Enlightenment and Despair: A History of Sociology*, 2nd ed. (Cambridge University Press, 1987) contains a sustained treatment of the impact of the Enlightenment and its focus on reasoning on subsequent social theorizing. Immanuel Wallerstein's *Unthinking Social Science: The Limits of Nineteenth-Century Paradigms* (Blackwell, 1991) helps to contextualize these theories historically within the development of mercantilism, colonialism, and industrial capitalism.

Irving Zeitlin, in his *Ideology and the Development of Sociological Theory*, 5th ed. (Prentice-Hall, 1994), 1–45, briefly discusses some of the important Enlightenment thinkers and details the debate between Rousseau and Wollstonecraft. For a contextualized discussion of Adam Smith, see Louis Schneider's edition of *The Scottish Moralists on Human Nature and Society* (University of Chicago Press, 1967).

Delving into Enlightenment epistemology can be a daunting task. One starting point is Carl J. Friedrich's edition of *The Philosophy of Kant: Immanuel Kant's Moral and Political Writings* (Modern Library, 1977). My understanding and development of the ERCA epistemological model were, oddly enough, first inspired by, and then adapted from, a conservative Jesuit philosopher's grappling with Kant and the Enlightenment: I continue to recommend Bernard J.F. Lonergan's *Insight* contained in *Collected Works of Bernard Lonergan*, vol. 3 (University of Toronto Press, 1988), despite and because of its conservative insights. For an excellent review of current neuroscientific and philosophical debates around conscious experience and human uniqueness, see David J. Chalmers, "The Puzzle of Conscious Experience," *Scientific American*, Dec. 1995, 80–86.

Finally, Rosalind A. Sydie's *Natural Women, Cultured Men: A Feminist Perspective on Sociological Theory* (UBC Press, 1994) gives an excellent feminist critique of Enlightenment thinkers and of the major classical social theorists. Edward W. Said's *Culture and Imperialism* (Alfred A. Knopf, 1993) discusses the context of colonialism and racism during the period considered in this text.

Suggestions for Research or Debate

1. What would a pre-Enlightenment European epistemology look like? Would each of its aspects be the polar opposite of an Enlightenment epistemology? How is pre-Enlightenment European thinking still prevalent?
2. Did the Enlightenment lead to the industrial/bourgeois/liberal democratic revolutions or vice versa? To what degree did the Enlightenment promote the larger social transformations? To what degree did the Enlightenment justify the limited emancipation that resulted from these revolutions?
3. Based on your own experiences, apply the ERCA model to an inter-personal relationship you have had and to your immediate class-room experience in this course. Does it make sense? How would you change the model?
4. Compare the degree of class and gender bias in Rousseau's and Wollstonecraft's Enlightened education programs. What other biases are apparent?
5. Compare an alternative, non-European world-view to the Enlightenment. What are the difficulties in even attempting to do so? Can these difficulties be overcome to some degree at least?

The Enlightenment and Value-Stances on Humans, Existing Society, and the Possibility of Radical Social Change

TWO

In the previous chapter we discussed aspects of the Enlightenment in order to introduce a first organizing principle for our subsequent discussion of classical social theory: an Enlightened epistemological model. In this chapter we continue to focus on the Enlightenment in order to introduce the other central organizing principle in this text: the existence in all social theorizing of definite value-stances with respect to human potential, existing societal organization, and the possibility of radical social change.

Enlightenment thinkers all shared a view that human beings (or at least some men) were potentially perfectible because of a unique ability to reason through conscious experience. This view was in direct opposition to prevailing doctrines such as the Christian position that we are all fundamentally flawed by the original sin of Adam and Eve. Rejecting the old belief that we required salvation by a heavenly Lord, Enlightenment thinkers tended to place their faith in the possibilities inherent in human reasoning.

If we are so perfectible, why, then, do we not live in a world of perfection? Again, Enlightenment thinkers tended to agree in their preliminary answer to this obvious question. We were not yet anywhere near perfection because of the tremendous social constraints on our freedom to reason, constraints that had become embedded in all existing forms of societal organization. In other words, the principal problem that was barring human *progress* towards liberty, equality, and solidarity was located in social organization, not in some fatal flaw in human nature.

For relative conservatives such as Kant, the inability of reasoners to reason in public without fear of negative social sanctions was the "only" social organizational problem. Liberal-radicals such as Rousseau pointed to coercive political and economic constraints that had developed under pre-Enlightened conditions of undemocratic authoritarianism. Again, despite differences in the perceived extent and depth of the social problem, all liberal-radical thinkers viewed existing social organization to be fundamentally negative for human development. Radical or fundamental social change was necessary to unchain human potential.

But if human beings were not fatally flawed, how did such "bad" forms of social organization appear and become so systemic or structurally embedded? Rousseau's *Discourse on the Origins of Inequality* exemplifies one Enlightened liberal-radical response to this conundrum. In that work, Rousseau speculates on what human nature might have been without social constraints ("natural man" in individuated, indifferent harmony with all other nature and humans). Only scarcities and population increases must have driven "man" into early forms of social organization and sociability. Social interaction unleashed our natural potential to reason and led to advances in human enjoyment and security, culminating in plant cultivation, animal husbandry, and a division of labour.

With these "natural" developments arose notions of nature as privatized property as well as forms of the state to protect these socially divisive property rights. It was this seemingly natural introduction of privatized property that, Rousseau argued, basically structured intrasocietal inequality (like that between the rich and the poor), intersocietal divisions in human solidarity (such as wars), and the resultant lack of reasoning in humanity.

So, if we are not flawed by our very nature but by forms of societal organization that are unequal and divisive, what can possibly be done? As we have seen, for liberal-radical Enlightenment thinkers, social change was required in almost all aspects of societal organization. Such extensive social change was seen to be possible in a relatively gradual process of legislated reforms under the most propitious of conditions. In *The Social Contract*, for instance, Rousseau argued strongly for a program of extensive social, political, and cultural change. The existing state's authoritarian and anti-democratic organization was to be replaced with "popular sovereignty" in a wide range of forms. Only "physical inequality" was to remain legitimate; all other inequalities— moral, political, and otherwise—were to be delegitimized over time.

Symptomatic of the social-intellectual limitations of even the most apparently radical of Enlightenment thinkers, Rousseau confused physical differences (in size and so on) for justifiable "physical inequality" and, thereby, continued to condone a variety of racist and sexist responses to who was fully human. Even more symptomatic of the limitations of Enlightenment radicalism was Rousseau's inclusion of "inequality of property" as a justifiable, "natural" "physical inequality."

His own argument had pointed to privatized property as the central socially constructed, if apparently natural, chain around human development.

If we understand "radical" change in its most basic meaning of fundamental or "root" change, then we can conclude that Rousseau's programmatic analysis of the possibility for radical social change through popular sovereignty, under the guidance of Enlightened legislators, is not nearly as radical as his critique of existing societal organization might lead us to believe. Indeed, his unquestioning acceptance of property inequalities as non-social, physical inequality in *The Social Contract* is inconsistent with his stated view of high human potential and with his highly negative view of societal organization developed in his *Discourse on the Origin of Inequality*.

In the end, like Adam Smith and the other liberal-radical Enlightenment thinkers, Rousseau's bourgeois liberalism, so evident in his glorification of property inequality as natural, meant that he was a radical with respect to his critique of existing feudal social organization, but merely a reformist with respect to emerging capitalism. Liberty, equality, and solidarity remained dependent upon, and limited by, the possession of privatized property and the maintenance and expansion of private property rights.

As summarized in Table 2.1, Rousseau's highly positive view of human beings allowed for the eventual perfectibility of humanity. His generally negative view of current society as unreasonable enslavement underpinned his critical stance on all existing social organization. However, his unwillingness or inability to extend his critique of society to what he continued to conceive of as natural inequalities meant that the path to human perfectibility would be only gradual and would have to be guided by an elite of (white, European, wealthy) reasoning men, supposedly on behalf of all humanity.

Rousseau's Enlightenment stance contains the seeds of all three major approaches to social reasoning that were to emerge within classical social theory: the *elite engineering*, the *human emancipation*, and the *middle road* approaches. The elite engineering approach stressed the legitimate right of (and need for) a few good reasoners to guide society in a direction that was in the best interests of the not-yet-enlightened many. This approach was the first of the three to develop and has most often dominated academic social theorizing. In direct contradiction to elite engineering, a human emancipation approach emerged that stressed the potential of all human beings, was willing to treat all social inequalities as not primarily natural, and called for radical societal transformation by the reasoning majority. A third approach, the middle road, sought, perhaps like Rousseau most intended, to find a guided, gradualist way out of social enslavement without radical social change.

TABLE 2.1

Rousseau's Stance on Humans, Existing Societal Organization, and the Possibility of Radical Social Change

Human potential	Highly positive—humanity seen as perfectible (High +)
Existing societal organization	Negative—existing society is enslavement, but some inequalities, such as class, gender, and race, are deemed necessary (–)
Possibility of radical social change	Somewhat positive, under proper conditions and guidance and only if gradual (Weak +)

Like the best of Enlightenment thinking, all subsequent social theorizing contains a definite view of humanity, of existing societal organization, and of the necessity and possibility of radical social change. These views may be explicitly stated, and evidence may be accumulated to support them. On the other hand, viewpoints on human potential, society, and radical social change may be unstated or presumed, or may simply be asserted. Such untheorized views are mere value-assertions, instead of being value-assertions that are well theorized and argued for. While all social theorizing includes these value-assertions, the best theorizing makes them explicit and grounds them in rigorous analysis.

In everyday life, and not just in sociology classrooms, our own thinking about both "big" and "little" social issues also, maybe even necessarily, contains our responses to views on humanity, social organization, and radical social change. If, initially, we were to restrict our own response to each viewpoint to a simple positive or negative, then we would quickly make explicit, in a preliminary way, our general value-stance in making sense of the social world. In terms of the ERCA model, we would discover what value-choices we make on the basis of our prior reasoning. Then we could begin to determine to what degree these choices have "fed back" to influence our prior reasoning about social interactions, settings, and organizations and have directly influenced our actions. With this hindsight, we could then assess our current thinking about the social world in order to clarify our own inclinations and unreasonable blind spots in reasoning, choosing, and acting.

TABLE 2.2
Summary Table of the Eight Possible Stances in Social
Theorizing

Stances	Human potential	Existing societal organization	Possibility of radical social change
1	+	+	+
2	+	+	−
3	+	−	+
4	+	−	−
5	−	−	−
6	−	−	+
7	−	+	−
8	−	+	+

Becoming more aware of our own value-stance(s) would not only place us solidly on the path to better theorizing our own life process; it would also aid us in gaining insights into other people's value-stances and social theorizing. These other people's stances include, of course, those of our friends and enemies, as well as the theorizing of the great classical social theorists.

By restricting the allowable responses to each of the three views to simple affirmations or denials, we can chart the eight possible value-stances in social theorizing, as can be seen in Table 2.2. Some of these value-stances will certainly seem bizarre. My personal favourite in the category of the bizarre is Stance 1 (+ + +), which can be translated as: "Humans can be so much more than we currently are; current societal social organization is nearly perfect; let's make revolution!" Other stances may seem frightening, even suicidal. The sobering point is that there almost certainly are adherents to each stance. Even more sobering is the recognition of how often some people, including ourselves, change value-stances without reasoning why. And maybe most sobering of all is the recognition that some people, at least, seem to cling adamantly to their value-stance despite its contradictions in the face of solid, conflicting evidence.

Whatever your stance, it is important to realize that what may well seem obvious and the best position to you does not necessarily mean it will seem so to others. Indeed, the fact that it may seem obvious and best to your friends, or to a majority or small minority of public opinion, does not mean it is "correct" or "incorrect." A value-stance is necessary, but not suffficient, for insightful social theorizing.

As the Enlightenment would have it, the closer we can get to reasoning towards our choices, the closer we can get to informed action.

The crux of insightful social theorizing is located in the relative reasonability of the arguments adduced. Solid social theorizing lies in insightfulness or reasonability of the specific arguments regarding the level of human potential, the equality of existing social organization, and the possibility of radical change.

For example, Rousseau's great worth, or lack of worth, as a social thinker is not determined by his having taken, to a degree, Stance 3 (+ – +). As was implicit in our discussion of his key works, his insight is much better assessed by means of a critical evaluation of how well he argued in favour of high human potential, against existing societal organization, and for the strong necessity for radical social change, and by how consistent his analysis of the possibility of such change was with his other arguments. In the end, Rousseau's particular contributions to enduring social theorizing are best assessed comparatively, in relationship to other theorists of Stance 3 and then in relation to other theorists of whatever stance.

Each of the following chapters on specific theorists and approaches contains a brief identification of the underlying value-stance and epistemological (ERCA) model used by the theorist. As well each chapter focuses, in more extended depth, on critically examining an array of evidence offered in the theorist's own written works in support of each aspect of that value-stance. In this process, we will discover that most of classical social theory is a collision between Stances 3 (emancipation), 4 (the middle road), and 7 (elite engineering). Within this collision, each classical social theorist advanced strong, vital arguments and attempted to bring forward solid evidence in support of one particular stance. In the course of their writings, a few classical social theorists even changed their stance on the basis of what they believed to be better evidence for an alternative stance. For a change, investigating classical social theory, all of which theorizes social change, is well worth the effort.

Key Sources

Johan Heilbron's *The Rise of Social Theory* (University of Minnesota Press, 1995) ably situates the early development of social theory. The history of the modern notion of progress is traced in J.B. Bury's *The Idea of Progress: An Inquiry into Its Growth and Origin* (Dover, 1960).

Rousseau's *Discourse on the Origin of Inequality* and *The Social Contract* are in *The Social Contract and other Discourses* (E.P. Dutton, 1950).

I am not aware of any other text that summarizes social theorizing in a similar manner to the present text. The original edition of Irving Zeitlin's text, referred to in chapter 1, inspired me to examine classical social theory in the context of "ideological" debates.

Suggestions for Research and Debate

1. Critically evaluate the inconsistencies between Rousseau's *Discourse on the Origin of Inequality* and *The Social Contract*. Speculate on what a more consistent argument might contain.

2. Identify and evaluate your own value-stance as it was utilized in a recent friendly conversation, a recent argument, and in an argument you had a few years ago. What lessons for better theorizing can you draw?

3. Identify the value-stance that seems most bizarre to you. Attempt to argue that it is a solid stance. In the process, attempt to identify some of the political, economic, social, and cultural biases that made that stance seem so bizarre.

4. Identify a value-stance that is not your own but that seems that it might be intriguing to pursue. Again, attempt to identify some of the political, economic, social, and cultural biases that keep you from accepting it.

Elite Engineering I:
Auguste Comte's Positivism
and the "Reformist" Origins
of Sociology

Auguste Comte (1798–1857) coined the term *sociology* after he discovered that his preferred term, *social physics*, had already been used by a Belgian statistician. Never a particularly humble man, Comte sought to construct the complete theoretical-methodological framework within which the supreme form of knowledge, *positivism*, was to reach its apex in the most complete scientific discipline, his social physics. Comte's positivistic science of social physics is commonly recognized to be the first systematized sociological theory. Because he is taken to be the defining "father" of sociology, we need to examine carefully just what his sociology entails.

Comte was born in Montpellier, France, to reactionary, Catholic, monarchist, middle-class parents within a decade of the French Revolution of 1789, a revolution that had asserted liberty, equality, and solidarity and that had attempted, at least initially, to replace both the monarchy and institutional Catholicism with Enlightened popular sovereignty. As is the case with all of the other theorists examined in this text, fascinating, heuristic (eureka-helping) insights into the motivational bases for Comte's social theorizing can certainly be gleaned through detailed analysis of the interrelationships between his ideas and their specific historical and biographical contexts. Indeed, it is often difficult not to reduce the insights of individuals to a straightforward ideological reaction to their personal lives and political times. In the case of Comte, such experience included a turbulent personal life marked by depressions and certified "madness," and the prevailing turmoil associated with political and economic struggles during the rise of industrial capitalism in France.

In this text, our primary focus is on introducing and situating various key reasoning concepts within the approach of each theorist and relating them to both the epistemological and ideological models presented in the first two chapters. Then, and after much further research, serious students of social theory can interpret for themselves to what extent a given theory is merely ideological and to what degree it actually illuminates the social world. Here, we will simply note that Comte was deeply motivated by what he saw to be the "intellectual chaos" and "moral anarchy" of modern times, especially in his native France.

Comte derived his initial views on the centrality of science and industry from both his attendance at France's prestigious Ecole Polytehnique in Paris and from a lengthy stint as secretary and research assistant to one of France's best-known reformist philosophers and glorifiers of the new industrial and scientific era, Henri de Saint-Simon. Unlike Saint-Simon, Comte saw a need to reorganize all knowledge systematically and hierarchically, as the necessary and seemingly sufficient "spiritual" prelude to the institutionalization of a new social stability upon the ruins of anarchic, industrial society.

This he proceeded to do at length, and to his own abundant satisfaction, in *The Positive Philosophy* (1830–42). Comte believed that his most central "discovery" was what he termed the invariable *law of three stages*. For him, all knowledge and all societies gradually and progressively develop from a "theological" or "fictitious" stage through a briefer, transitional, and chaotic "metaphysical" or "abstract" stage, towards the ultimate "scientific" or "positive" stage.

> From the study of the development of human intelligence, in all directions, and through all times, the discovery arises of a great fundamental law, to which it is necessarily subject, and which has a solid foundation of proof, both in the facts of our organization and in our historical experience. The law is this: that each of our leading conceptions—each branch of our knowledge—passes successively through three different theoretical conditions: the Theological or fictitious; the Metaphysical, or abstract; and the Scientific, or positive. In other words, the human mind, by its nature, employs in its progress three methods of philosophizing, the character of which is essentially different, and even radically opposed: viz., the theological method, the metaphysical, and the positive. Hence arise three philosophies, or general systems of conception on the aggregate of phenomena, each of which excludes the others. The first is the necessary point of departure of the human understanding; and the third is its fixed and definite state. The second is merely a state of transition.
>
> In the theological state, the human mind, seeking the essential nature of beings, the first and final causes (the origin and purpose) of all effects—in short, Absolute knowledge—supposes all phenomena to be produced by the immediate action of supernatural beings.
>
> In the metaphysical state, which is only a modification of the first, the mind supposes, instead of supernatural beings, abstract forces, veritable

entitities (that is, personified abstractions) inherent in all beings, and capable of producing all phenomena. What is called the explanation of phenomena is, in this stage, a mere reference of each to its proper entity.

In the final, the positive stage, the mind has given over the vain search after Absolute notions, the origin and destination of the universe, and the causes of phenomena, and applies itself to the study of laws—that is, their invariable relations of succession and resemblance. Reasoning and observation, duly combined, are the means of this knowledge. What is now understood when we speak of an explanation of facts is simply the establishment of a connection between single phenomena and some general facts, the number of which continually diminishes with the progress of science.

Thus, societies and knowledges that are rooted in beliefs in the cohesion and causality of a fictitious supernatural order become, everywhere and over time, temporarily replaced by metaphysical or abstract negative/critical philosophical principles rooted in supposed human nature. Finally and forever, negative metaphysical societies are to be superseded by positive, scientific societies dominated by principles derived from empirical induction.

As a way of demystifying positivism, it is perhaps useful to recall three meanings of "being positive," all of which were conflated in Comte's supposedly strictly objective usage. A first meaning of being positive is "positing," in the sense of proposing or putting forward: "I posit that the earth goes around the sun." A second meaning connotes certitude: "I'm positive that your answer is correct." And a third connotation implies being neither negative nor neutral but being willingly in favour: "He has a very positive attitude about studying."

Comte argued that positivist science was a higher stage of development than either theology or metaphysics, because its laws were based upon generalizations from induction, not deduction from the supernatural or from merely abstract principles. For Comte, only the rigorous application of his understanding of induction in the sciences could allow relatively certain knowledge. Only scientific (positing and empirically observed) knowledge could provide the certain, solid basis for predicting subsequent events and, by means of that prediction, the ability to control future occurrences. Comte's most famous dictum captures this general positivist and instrumentalist ideology: "Savoir pour prevoir et prevoir pour pouvoir."

But Comte was concerned not just with replacing what he thought to be deduction with what he took to be the proper business of science, lawmaking, and instrumental control through induction. Comte, of course, was attempting to enunciate the principles upon which all sciences would become increasingly based; but he also wanted to discover and found a new and "superior" science of social physics or sociology in order to govern societal development.

His *hierarchy of sciences* established, again to his own satisfaction, his kind of sociology as the highest form of positivist science. In *The Positive Philosophy*, Comte arranged the "basic" sciences in a rank-ordering according to their levels of inherent complexity, immediacy to human activity, and length of time taken to become a positivist science. Thus, for Comte, the (mechanical) physical sciences were the least inherently complex, furthest from human activity, and first rooted in positivist principles. The biological sciences were intermediate and built upon the (mechanical) physical sciences. Sociology or social physics, the science that Comte claimed was his greatest invention, was the most complex, the closest to human activity, and therefore the last to be positivized—by Comte! Once sociology had been positivized, all of science could be unified into his positive philosophy. This philosophy would then be the instrument to control the creation of a fully positive society.

Just as the biological sciences were built upon the findings and approaches of the physical sciences, sociology was, where appropriate, to be built on the findings and approaches of the biological sciences of his time. The *organismic* logic of biology and its stress on statics (anatomy) first and then dynamics (physiology) provided the basic framework for Comtean sociology (and, as we will see, of a great deal of later sociology). A focus on how the parts of society are related to the whole organism and serve its life was taken to be the central focus of sociology. Structure and function were seen to determine process. The whole took precedence and gave coherence to the parts.

With the aid of his law of three stages and his hierarchy of sciences and consequent biological, organismic logic, Comte could finally launch his frontal attack on the major Enlightenment value-position (Stance 3, + − +). In order to establish his kind of social theory (positivist), he had to attack the "negativism" embedded in the extensive critiques of existing social organization by, especially, the most radical of the Enlightenment *philosophes*.

As we have seen, in his law of three stages he replaced Enlightened negativism about society with a positive attitude towards the higher stage of positivistic society that he saw emerging from the chaos of the declining metaphysical stage under the direction of his positivist philosophy. Negativism about society was, in other words, increasingly to be seen as a backward step in societal development. Comte's positivism was both a scientific stance of positing and attaining relative certitude *and* a positive attitude towards the reform of existing society (+) through an elite's application of positivist principles.

But to establish his positivism as a social theory above Enlightened

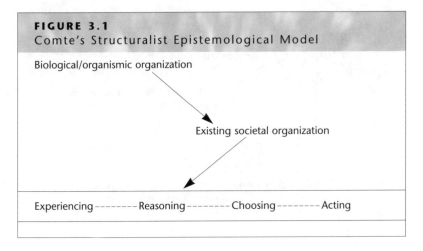

FIGURE 3.1
Comte's Structuralist Epistemological Model

Biological/organismic organization

Existing societal organization

Experiencing --------- Reasoning --------- Choosing --------- Acting

negativism, Comte also had to negate the highly positive (in the third sense, favourable) view of the creative potential of human beings that was crucial to Enlightened negativism. This was accomplished by applying a structuralist metalogic to the organismic analogy he derived from the biology of his times. For Comte, the idea and ideal of society was the real object of analysis in the new sociology: the real organism to be explained and developed. The only appropriate units of social analysis were said to be progressively more complex forms of social structural organization, the simplest and earliest form of social structural organization being the family.

Comte argued that these structurally ordered units were the only real organs of the societal organism. Individual human beings, like the ones the Enlightenment had championed, were mere "abstractions," unreal figments of metaphysical imagination. Indeed, the Comtean hierarchy of sciences denied social psychology any "basic" validity. What appeared as individuality—including one's experiences, reasonings, choices, and actions—was viewed by Comte as fully determined by biology and by existing social organization. All "affective," "cognitive," and "active" human attributes were seen as determined, in the long run, by the general development of society (see Figure 3.1).

Since individual human beings were not really real and, therefore, were without rights as such (–), Enlightenment claims for human emancipation were seen by Comte as entirely "egoistic" and "vain" and as socially backward. As society became increasingly governed by positivist principles, individuality would gradually attain socially positive attitudes such as "attachment," "veneration," and "universal love." "Abstract" individuals would become a single, "real" humanity.

According to the law of three stages, social organization was already

TABLE 3.1

Comte's Stance on Humans, Existing Societal Organization, and the Possibility of Radical Social Change

Human potential	Highly negative—human beings seen as abstractions (High –)
Existing societal organization	Highly positive and positivist (High +)
Possibility of radical social change	Impossible—guided positive evolutionary reforms only (High –)

becoming positivist. This process would be greatly facilitated, Comte reckoned, by the dissemination of his positive philosophy. Radical societal social change was, therefore, totally unnecessary (–). Indeed, since the positive stage was supposed to be the last stage of societal development, radical social change was impossible (–). Only gradual progress was possible, and only if guided by positive philosophy.

In *The Positive Philosophy* Comte had countered theoretically the value-stance of the Enlightenment (+ – +) with its polar opposite (– + –). The completion of history would be when all humanity was one society under the guidance of positive philosophy. All that was required was the gradual implementation of Auguste Comte's positivism so that his "Ideas" could "govern the world."

> The Positive Philosophy offers the only solid basis for that Social Reorganization which must succeed the critical condition in which the most civilized nations are now living.
>
> It cannot be necessary to prove to anybody who reads this work that Ideas govern the world, or throw it into chaos; in other words, that all social mechanism rests upon Opinions. The great political and moral crisis that societies are now undergoing is shown by a rigid analysis to arise out of intellectual anarchy. While stability in fundamenal maxims is the first condition of genuine social order, we are suffering under an utter disagreement which may be called universal. Till a certain number of general ideas can be acknowledged as a rallying-point of social doctrine, the nations will remain in a revolutionary state, whatever palliatives may be devised; and their institutions can be only provisional. But whenever the necessary agreement on first principles can be obtained, appropriate institutions will issue from them, without shock or resistance; for the causes

of disorder will have been arrested by the mere fact of the agreement. It is in this direction that those must look who desire a natural and regular, a normal state of society.

That Comtean positivist and structuralist social theory was not merely, or even primarily, scientific becomes more readily apparent in his later works, *A General View of Positivism* (1849) and *System of Positive Polity* (1851–54). In *A General View* Comte announced, with his characteristic lack of circumspection, that the objective of his positive philosophy was "to direct the spiritual reorganization of the civilized world," and "to construct the system of morality under which the final regeneration of Humanity will proceed." We have already seen that this intention was at least implicit in his earlier "objectivity."

In his *System* Comte detailed exactly what the new positivist society, based on the application of his positive philosophy of moral regeneration, would entail and how it could be successfully engineered. There, in his final major work, he invented yet another science to supersede sociology at a new, even more "spiritual" level of analysis—the "science of morals." He gave precise instructions for how to organize this new "science" internationally into "the religion of humanity" by means of a "positivistic church" based in Paris, and headed by himself as the first "high priest." Thus, Comte's last work is filled with exactly the metaphysics and theological dogma that he had railed against so strongly in his earlier writings.

By the 1850s, Comte had realized that his positive philosophy was capturing support away from neither the liberal nor the socialist progeny of the Enlightenment and the French Revolution. His new positivistic church was, therefore, designed to vanquish this progeny ideologically and politically. For him, liberal democracy was the domination of society by those of uncontrolled greed and little intellect. Socialism, on the other hand, lacked any appreciation of what Comte saw to be innate inequalities in humanity. Moreover, socialism underplayed the need for harmony based on the subordination and control of the population through "firm" "moral force."

In his final works, Comte returned full circle to the theological stage he had formerly dismissed as so immature. Comte's model of the new spiritual order was rooted in a reconceptualization of the reactionary Catholic social theories of Louis de Bonald and Joseph de Maistre. These anti-Enlightenment thinkers had, in fact, earlier inspired both his structural realism and his organismic logic. In the end, they also inspired his retreat to a highly romanticized medieval Europe in which the polity was both separate from and dominated by the church and its "universal" ideology. Comtean positivism had clearly become the new "catholic" theology to confront Enlightened negativism, rather than the science it had purported to be.

The increasingly bizarre development of Auguste Comte's social theorizing may motivate many readers not to treat his work seriously. This would be a major error. Comte's positivism pervades most of classical (and much of contemporary) social theorizing. The "objective," strictly "scientific" guise of positivism often hides its positively ideological underpinnings more successfully than did its founding father's formulations. Knowing the Comtean roots of positivism will serve you well in identifying such supposed objectivity.

Equally important, the social structural-realist argument and its organismic logic were directly taken up by later theorists, most notably Emile Durkheim, to refine and advance a more sophisticated version of Comte's value stance (– + –). Structural realism is, in fact, probably the most common metatheory in social analysis. Humans are most often viewed as mere results or vectors of structured social forces, even by many theorists who purport to be diametrically opposed to Comte's conservative social reformism.

Thirdly, Comte's repeated and transparent attempts to establish positivism, structural realism, *and* his conservative value stance as the only acceptable, legitimate grounds for social analysis and, therefore, societal reform is, perhaps, only slightly less frighteningly anti-democratic than his principles concerning how to control the reformation of existing society through an elite's application of these principles. Today, like yesterday, there is a burgeoning elite of technocrats who justify what they do on the basis of positivist principles and who repeatedly deny democratic involvement on the basis that only "they" know what is good for "us."

Comte's hierarchical law of the three stages of proper knowledges and societies should again alert us to the profound Eurocentric and imperialistic roots of social theorizing and of sociology in general. Besides directly discrediting non-positivistic knowledges and forms of social organization, Comte consistently viewed women and non-whites as less capable of positivism and, thus, of development. For the defining father of sociology, only the "white race," led by white, upper-class men, could attain for "humanity" the pure light of positivism.

Key Sources

Auguste Comte's major works are *The Positive Philosophy* (AMS Press, 1974), *A General View of Positivism* (Robert Speller and Sons, 1957), and *System of Positive Polity* (Burt Franklin, 1976). Kenneth Thompson's edition of *Auguste Comte: The Foundation of Society* (Wiley, 1975) provides a broad selection from these works.

A.R. Standley's *Auguste Comte* (Twayne, 1981), and Boris Sokoloff's

The "Mad" Philosopher Auguste Comte (Greenwood Press, 1975) are good secondary sources on Comte's life and work. Frank E. Manuel's *The Prophets of Paris* (Harper and Row, 1965) places Comte in the context of Saint-Simon and others. A fine chapter-length treatment of Comte, linking his ideas to Bonald and de Maistre, is in David Ashley and David M. Orenstein's *Sociological Theory: Classical Statements*, 3rd ed. (Allyn and Bacon, 1995), 68–101.

Suggestions for Research and Debate

1. Identify three examples of positivism in a recent issue of a sociological journal. To what degree is the positivism pervasive throughout that issue? To what degree are all three meanings of positivism pervasive in your examples and in the entire issue of the journal?
2. Identify three examples of structuralism in a recent issue of a sociological journal. To what degree is it pervasive throughout that issue? To what degree is social structural-realism linked to positivism?
3. Identify three examples of elite-led social engineering in your immediate environment. To what degree are members of the elite proponents of positivism and of social structural-realism?
4. Debate the following proposition: "All sociology is doomed because its defining 'father' was such a despotic fanatic."
5. Try to develop a positivist answer to the question, "If society is not yet perfect and humans are mere abstractions of societal reality, how does a positivist elite deserving of complete trust arise?"
6. To what extent have twentieth-century developments in the physical and biological sciences damaged the validity of Comte's organismic logic in the social sciences?

Emancipation Ia:
Karl Marx's Historical
Materialism and the
Problem of Human
Alienation

FOUR

Karl Marx (1818–83) grew up in Trier, Germany, in a prosperous and Enlightened household. Two years before Karl's birth, his father had converted from Judaism to Protestantism in order to enhance his income as a lawyer and to hold public office. Karl married his next-door sweetheart, Jenny, the daughter of a wealthy, liberal follower of Saint-Simon, Baron von Westphalen, and received a doctorate in philosophy at the University of Berlin. The "good life" was there for the taking. Instead, Marx was blacklisted from ever attaining a professorial post at a university because of his radical political activities and was forced into exile in France, then in Belgium, and finally in England. In London, as elsewhere, Karl Marx and his family often lived in destitution, dependent on petty earnings from journalism and Jenny's labour, and on the stipend that his close comrade Frederick Engels sporadically supplied to him.

In this context, and often with Engels as secondary author, Marx produced the single most important body of writing in modern revolutionary social theory. Certainly no other social theorist, revolutionary or otherwise, has had such global and controversial impact on both the academic and larger social worlds.

Marx's entire body of work—his "Marxism"—is the first, the foundational, modern social theory of societal change. Because of their sheer number, depth, and range, Marx's writings are best viewed holistically, as developing over time. One standard way to do this, which we follow, is to explore his work in three parts. These are held to be roughly coincident with his life—the "humanist" and "philosophical" Early Marx; the "political," "sociological," and "historical" Middle Marx; and the "political-economic" and "objective" Later Marx—although the writings of the so-called Middle and Later Marx were in fact interspersed throughout his middle and later life.

The current chapter examines the major writings of the young, so-called humanist and philosophical Early Marx in order to discuss his crucial and abiding concepts that were developed, in the first instance, out of his view of human potential. The next chapter examines Marx's insights into understanding and explaining existing societal organization, drawing from sources by the "Later Marx." A third chapter examines his understanding of the possibility of revolutionary social transformation towards socialism and communism, and draws upon the so-called Middle Marx. By paying careful attention to all three periods, we will discover the fundamental unity of Marx's social theory and why it has had such persistent impact.

Marx accepted that, within philosophy, Georg Wilhelm Friedrich Hegel (1770–1831) had transcended Immanuel Kant's absolute divide between spirit and matter and his consequent radical "indifference" to the real world. Hegel's philosophy, unlike Kant's, initially attracted the young Marx precisely because of its holistic unification of spirit and matter in human history and, following from this, its human emancipatory potential through the critical unification of theory and practice. However, for Marx, Hegel's supersedence of Kantianism had itself to be transcended, along with all abstract philosophy, because, in the first instance, of its inherently uncritical conservatism.

Whereas Kantianism underpinned an Enlightened, liberal/bourgeois celebration of atomized individualism, Hegelianism superseded the selfish individuation inherent in the everyday socio-economic relations of bourgeois *civil society* by viewing human history as a progressive, though uneven, unfolding of "Mind" or "Spirit" through increasingly self-reflective human "Reason." Hegel's *dialectical idealism* was basically an ongoing, contradictory, and interrelational process by which humans attempted to become reasonable—more like Mind or Spirit—through "the negation of the negation," the movement to more self-reflective reasoning by overcoming contradiction.

According to Hegel, this dialectical (ongoing, interrelational, and contradictory) unfolding of Spirit would gradually subordinate both "the domain of particular altruism," or group identification, that characterized former historical times as well as "the domain of universal egoism" in bourgeois civil society with "the domain of universal altruism" in which the whole community's "general will" is completely expressed through "the State." The Word, as it were, becomes flesh in the State, subordinating civil society and "corporation" interests and thereby ensuring freedom for all. In his later years, Hegel increasingly identified the militaristic Prussian state of his time as the highest form of Spirit incarnate.

Following the lead of his fellow Young Hegelian, Ludwig Feuerbach, Marx rather quickly came to realize that Hegelian conservatism was situated and sustained by *idealism*, the treatment of material reality as if it were determined by pre-existing idea-categories. By 1843 Marx had borrowed Feuerbach's *humanism* and *materialist* (matter yields spirit) negation of Hegel's idealism (spirit yields matter) to argue, in *On the Jewish Question*, that the political emancipation of the State and of religion would not lead to human emancipation. Only the "universal emancipation" of civil society would lead to human emancipation *from* both the State and the privatized property rights that it so religiously sustains.

In *Introduction to the Critique of Hegel's Philosophy of Right* (1843), Marx continued to use Feuerbach's materialism and humanism to identify the primary material force in civil society that was able to create this universal human emancipation. Marx concluded that this force was the *proletariat*, a "universal class" whose "sufferings are universal," a class "which is, in short, a total loss of humanity and which can only redeem itself by a total redemption of humanity." Driven by material necessity, only the proletariat, all of those with no special interests to protect and with nothing to lose by social revolution, could produce "universal freedom" by freeing itself from "all" forms of "oppression."

By 1843, Marx had already identified himself as a materialist who had found the key for emancipation not in the sky of abstract ideas but in the everyday lives of the most humanly degraded, the proletariat. He had also introduced his lifelong expository method of vigorous, often scathing and always unremitting, critique of social reality and of ultimately apologetic interpretations of that reality.

The Economic and Philosophic Manuscripts of 1844 are justly famous for Marx's earliest conceptualization of the *alienation of the labour process*—the fundamental contradiction within existing bourgeois civil society from the point of view of human self-emancipation. In this work, Marx argues that, within existing civil society, people's life-defining human creativity, their "practical-critical" activity—that is, their labour—is, in reality, carried out under conditions in which their creative product "confronts" them "as *something alien*, as a *power independent* of the producers." Indeed, "in the conditions dealt with by political economy"— the conditions of bourgeois civil society—labour can only appear as "estrangement, as alienation," as apart from workers' creativity. The more the creator, or labourer, works, the "more powerful" the objectified world becomes and the more estranged and degraded the worker becomes. For instance, workers create the very privatized property that the owners utilize to extract even more of the workers' creativity.

Alienation from the product of one's practical creativity defines the entire process of production as alienating. "If then the product of labour is alienation, production itself must be active alienation, the alienation of activity, the activity of alienation." In bourgeois civil society, our human creativity, what for Marx distinguishes us from all other species, is used against us to divide us from ourselves, from other humans, and from the rest of the world around us. Our life-defining, human-emancipatory creativity becomes, in social reality, mere toil, mere drudgery; "in his work therefore, he does not affirm himself but denies himself, does not feel content but unhappy, does not develop freely his mental and physical energy but mortifies his body and ruins his mind." This practical human activity in its alienated form creates all seemingly external products, including private property.

In his *Theses on Feuerbach* (1845), Marx outlined the basic principles that distinguish his materialist approach from Feuerbach's "contemplative materialism." Marx condemns "all hitherto existing materialism (that of Feuerbach included)" for denying the absolute centrality of "sensuous human activity" or "practice" to "all social life." For Marx, only real human beings, and not abstracted ideas about them, transform the world through practical-critical or "revolutionary" activity. Indeed, for Marx, only the human species is capable of practical-critical personal and social transformation. "The coincidence of the changing of circumstances and of human activity or self-changing can be conceived and rationally understood only as *revolutionary practice*."

Whereas Hegel's idealism had rooted change in the gradual manifestation of the Spirit in history, Feuerbach's materialism objectified human practice by seeking a universal and ahistorical "human essence" in the atomized individual of bourgeois civil society. But, for Marx, "the human essence is no abstraction inherent in each single individual. In its reality it is the ensemble of the social relations." Thus, "the standpoint of the old materialism is civil society; the standpoint of the new is human society, or social humanity."

Social humanity changes over time and space through human practice, not by merely thinking about it. As Marx said: "Philosophers have only *interpreted* the world, in various ways; the point is to *change* it." Both the emancipation of practical-critical activity, or labour, from the confines of isolating and individuating civil society and the ongoing creation of social humanity can only be brought about by the practical-critical self-emancipation of labour from its contradictory confines. No elite of great thinkers or of great tinkerers who somehow purport to have risen above material reality can ever substitute for labour's self-emancipation.

Theses on Feuerbach clearly outlines Marx's general emancipatory epistemology and his, as opposed to Feuerbach's, humanism. As human beings, we produce both the social world and ourselves through our labour, through our practical-critical activity. The social relations that condition that activity are themselves a product of our social activity. These relations neither always were, nor will they always be, with us. They certainly condition our experiences, reasoning, choosing, and acting, but they do not completely determine them. In changing the social world through practical-critical action, we human beings regularly recreate ourselves by changing the social conditions in which we experience, reason, choose, and subsequently act again. We have no predetermined human nature except our unique ability to change our world through practical-critical action. By transforming the social world through revolutionary practice, we transform ourselves.

In Marx and Engels's *The Holy Family* (1845), Marx's general emancipatory epistemology and his humanism are further specified. In this work, Marx's conceptualization of the alienated labour process is linked dialectically to the identification of the proletariat as the key to emancipation, a position that Marx and Engels had each arrived at separately against Hegelian idealism. The proletariat and wealth are argued to be "antitheses," two sides of the same whole of private property that human labour has created and that are in opposition to each other. However, "Private property, as private property, as wealth, is forced to maintain its own existence and thereby the existence of its opposite, the proletariat.... The proletariat, on the other hand, is forced as proletariat, to abolish itself, and with this, its antithesis, the condition which makes it a proletariat—private property."

"The propertied class and the proletarian class express the same human alienation. But the former feels comfortable and confirmed in it, recognizes this self-alienation as *its own power* and thus has a *semblance* of a human existence. The latter feels itself crushed by this alienation, sees in it its own impotence and the reality of an inhuman existence." Experienced and understood necessity compels the proletariat, as opposed to wealth-holders, to choose to transform society and, thus, all of social humanity. Insofar as wealth-holders act as wealth-holders, they are compelled by their life-conditions to seek to maintain and enhance the basic social system of dehumanization.

Thus, Marx rooted his specific epistemology and humanism in his conceptualization of the fundamental class contradiction in actually existing society: the antithesis between wealth and the proletariat and the inability of wealth to move beyond itself. His epistemology is most centrally an epistemology for collective, proletarian self-emancipation through the collective self-development of revolutionary practice. His humanism is a humanism that is rooted in the conditions of actually existing class society.

Under conditions of classlessness that might be envisioned, all humans, would be unconstrained to develop the full scope of their practical-critical activity. Under conditions of bourgeois civil society, only the proletariat and its allies can and will transform society. The bourgeoisie will not transform capitalism and, indeed, cannot do so unless they were to cease being bourgeoisie. Alienated individual pro-

28

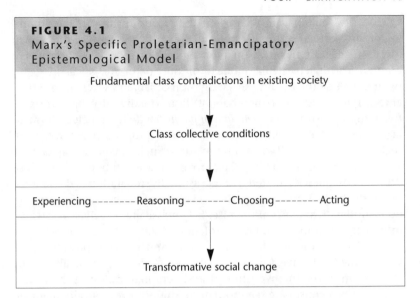

FIGURE 4.1
Marx's Specific Proletarian-Emancipatory
Epistemological Model

Fundamental class contradictions in existing society

Class collective conditions

Experiencing ------- Reasoning ------- Choosing ------- Acting

Transformative social change

29

letarians cannot as mere individuals transform capitalism, even when they so wished.

As diagrammed in Figure 4.1, Marx's specific proletarian-emancipatory epistemological model is that fundamental class contradictions in existing capitalist society lead to fundamentally different and opposing conditions of class collective life. Differing and opposing conditions of life lead to differing and opposing experiences, insights, choices, and actions. Only the abrogation of class contradictions will allow the emancipation of all humanity. But only the proletariat and its allies can and will tackle that emancipatory task.

In *The German Ideology* (1845–46) Marx and Engels finally lay the critical, philosophical groundwork for the full-fledged social theory that would later become *historical materialism*. In this work, the authors definitively distinguish their theoretical approach from Feuerbachian materialism, from Hegelian idealism, and from forms of "'true' socialism." Marx and Engels steadfastly argue against any form of *mechanistic materialism* that identifies human beings as nothing other than the passive products of uncontrollable circumstances. Such theories cannot account for how and why the mechanistic theorist could rise above the dross of total determination to identify those determining conditions and engineer their eradication on behalf of the mindless mass. Historical materialism, on the other hand, begins and ends with "the real individuals, their activity and the material conditions under which they live, both those which they find already existing and those produced by their activity."

Historical materialism focuses on the "world-historical" conditioning of any particular "mode of production" of "life, both of one's own in labour and of fresh life in procreation" in society. At any given moment within a particular mode of production of life, *productive forces* (which include the existing social division of labour as well as industrial techniques and the natural habitat) limit the diversity, or degrees of freedom, of existing social *relations of production* (which include formal-legal economic and political relations such as property rights, informal social relations, as well as cultural relations such as consciousness, reasoning, choosing, and acting). Yet, any given set of productive forces is itself a consequence of altered or, occasionally, revolutionized relations of production. Marx argued that revolutions in bourgeois societies occur under "two *practical* premises": 1) massively perceived necessity, in which alienation becomes "intolerable," given the chasm between the proletariat and wealth; and 2) social and material possibility, in which the productive forces are sufficiently developed to allow the eradication of the impoverishment and dehumanization of the proletariat. Both premises are seen to require the prior real development of a globalized bourgeoisie and proletariat.

In the final section of *The German Ideology*, "'true' socialists" are attacked for idealistically conceptualizing the "most reasonable" social order without ever rooting that new order in the real needs and situation of the proletariat. In *The Poverty of Philosophy* (1847), Marx brilliantly extended his critique of idealism and true socialism to encompass French *utopian socialists* such as Pierre Joseph Proudhon. Marx criticized Proudhon for ignoring the historically rooted, everyday material conditions of the destitute in favour of implanting from above a set of ideal principles that the proletariat would be expected to uphold.

By the time of the revolutions of 1848 in Europe, Marx had developed, in rudimentary form, a completely new conceptual framework for a theory of transformative social change. Both the framework and the emerging theory were rooted in the uniquely human potential to be productive or creative, to act upon one's reasoning and choices.

As presented in Table 4.1, Marx's new conceptual framework for historical materialism seemingly replicated, or extended, the bourgeois Enlightenment value stance (human potential +, existing societal organization –, possibility of radical social change +). It is therefore important to note that Marx did not share the Enlightenment's idealist belief in timeless, spaceless human nature. Moreover, he never justified property rights or any other form of oppression as natural; he was consistently revolutionary; and he did not compromise his value-stance with the introduction of contradictory elitist engineering principles.

Needless to say, Marx's conceptual framework (+ – +) is completely antithetical to Comte's founding sociological stance (– + –). Indeed,

TABLE 4.1

Marx's Stance on Humans, Existing Societal Organization, and the Possibility of Radical Social Change

Human potential	Highly positive view of practical-critical activity, especially by the proletariat (High +)
Existing societal organization	Highly negative—productive forces and social relations are in contradiction and are intolerable (High –)
Possibility of radical social change	Possible through class struggle by the proletariat (High +)

31

Marx viewed such a stance to be merely apologetic and, therefore, unable to deliver on its claims to science. For Marx, such an approach could at best deliver some interesting descriptive information. Because it could never rigorously question existing bourgeois forces and relations of production, but could only assume them as eternal, such a stance could never provide a historical explanation of social reality that went beyond its appearances.

Key Sources

A broad array of Hegel's admittedly difficult writings is contained in Frederick G. Weiss's edition of *The Essential Writings of Hegel* (Harper and Row, 1974). For commentaries, see Herbert Marcuse's *Reason and Revolution: Hegel and the Rise of Social Theory* (Beacon Press, 1969) and chapter 6 of David Ashley and David Michael Orenstein, *Sociological Theory: Classical Statements* (Allyn and Bacon, 1995).

All of the various writings by Marx and Engels that have been referred to in this chapter can be found in *Early Writings* (Penguin, 1974), *The German Ideology* (International Publishers, 1970), and *The Poverty of Philosophy* (Foreign Languages Publishing House, n.d.). I especially recommend the latter two works.

C.J. Arthur provides an excellent brief introduction to many of Marx's early writings in his Introduction to *The German Ideology*, cited above. David McLellan's *The Young Hegelians and Karl Marx* (Oxford University Press, 1969) and *Karl Marx: His Life and Thought* (Macmillan, 1973) are useful in terms of setting the context.

Suggestions for Research and Debate

1. Compare (and contrast) Comte's idealism, Hegel's idealism, and Proudhon's idealism. Does each form of idealism mistake the inter-relationship between ideas and action? Why or why not?
2. Apply Marx's concept of alienation to your life today. What does it capture? What does it leave out?
3. Is there still a fundamental contradiction between wealth and the proletariat in our society today? If not, why not? If so, is the contradiction deepening?
4. Use Marx's conceptual framework to identify some reasons why many readers of this text might not want to hear what Marx has to say.
5. Identify a piece of idealist analysis in your own writings. How might a historical materialist approach reconceptualize that analysis? Would it yield greater insight?

Emancipation Ib:
Marx's Political Economy
of Capitalism

FIVE

Like the works of the Early Marx, the historical materialism of the
Middle Marx and the Later Marx was, of course, anything but apologetic of existing social conditions or of intellectual justifications for
oppression. Indeed, all his work was directed at the combined problematic of discovering the "hidden" structural roots of systematically
alienating societal organization, on the one hand, and the conditions
and directions of successful revolutionary social change on the other.

In this chapter, we explore some central concepts in Marx's *critique
of political economy*,—that is, his critical analysis of the societal organization of capitalism as a historically developing whole structure of
social relations and social-material forces. If, in other words, human
potential, especially working-class potential, was being systematically
abused by historically produced social obstacles, what were the origins
and the real "inner workings" of that currently existing system of obstacles? What were the central features of the social-structural lock on
human, especially working-class, emancipation? How were they produced and how are they reproduced?

By the time they wrote *The Communist Manifesto* (1848), Marx and
Engels had clearly realized that the principal blockage to emancipatory
practice was the historical development of class societies, in which the
few systematically lived off the fruit of the labours of the many. The
consequent development within each type of class society of specific
class struggles over the products of labour was the principal immediate
cause of change in societal organization. Thus, "The history of all hitherto existing society is the history of class struggles." Indeed, "The
modern bourgeois society that has sprouted from the ruins of feudal
society has not done away with class antagonisms. It has but established new classes, new conditions of oppression, new forms of struggle in place of the old ones."

The principal new classes established, we have seen, were the proletarian (or working) and capitalist (or bourgeois) classes. They related to each other insofar as workers had nothing to sell but their ability to labour (*labour power*), which they sold to the capitalist class, who owned the means of production and thus lived off the labour power of the workers. The principal new conditions of oppression were: the continual push by capitalists to alter and expand the means of production under its ownership, and therefore the size of the proletariat under its control; and the reduction of all forms of control over the proletariat's labour power (such as moral and political controls used in feudal times) to apparently "merely economic," "free" market controls. Consequently, the principal new forms of struggle were those around paid work.

We have already seen that, for Marx, the unique potential of human beings lies in creative practice, the ability, at a given time and place and within a given set of social and other material conditions, to act upon reasoning and choices. In *Grundrisse: Foundations of the Critique of Political Economy* (1857–58), Marx extensively outlined the theoretical ground rules for what was intended to be a full-fledged critique of capitalist political economy. "To begin with, the question under discussion is material production. Individuals producing in a society, and hence the socially determined production of individuals, is of course the point of departure."

For Marx, humans had no set nature as such. They were both *social producers* of material goods and *social products* of their production (including, but by no means limited to, their own material production). Thus, the conditions for "the socially determined," as opposed to individually or naturally determined, "production of individuals" were to be discovered in the everydayness of economic life, of "individuals producing in a society" through their labour.

As best presented in *Grundrisse*, Marx's general "method of political economy," his "correct scientific method," was to abstract, from the concrete everydayness of individuals producing in civil society, a few purely structural or holistic concepts that might best capture the chief aspects of any given concrete society, or of any social relationship within it. His primary source for that everydayness was the British government's own Blue Books on the conditions of life in the workplaces and communities of the nation, which Marx examined in almost legendary detail at the British Museum. Marx then applied these purely structural concepts to historical or contemporary societies and processes to see what they illumined and what they hid. Always, there had to be a return to practical activity to test the validity and reliability of the concepts. He hoped that each return to practical activity would deepen and heighten the explanation of apparently separate events and would thereby enhance the choices for action of people, especially the most oppressed.

Throughout the development of his political economy, Marx held firm to the materialist principle that abstracting from and returning to individuated bourgeois civil society and its economic *base* would facilitate an explanation of any class society. He maintained that this method was much more effective than the usual idealist practice of understanding a society's ideological *superstructure* of legal, political, bureaucratic, and ideational institutions and relations in order to explain the real everyday life of civil society. In general, class societies and class struggles around our most basic, materially productive labour tended to define the superstructure, not the other way around. This was especially the case in capitalism, where control over labour power was continually being reduced to (apparently) merely economic forms. The point is made most bluntly by Marx in his Preface to *A Contribution to the Critique of Political Economy* (1859):

> In the social production of their existence, men inevitably enter into definite relations, which are independent of their will, namely relations of production appropriate to a given stage in the development of the material forces of production. The totality of these relations of production constitutes the economic structure of society, the real foundation, on which arises a legal and political superstructure and to which correspond definite forms of social consciousness. The mode of production of material life conditions the general process of social, political and intellectual life.

Superstructural concepts (such as "democracy" and "population") that are unqualified by class (in contrast to "bourgeois democracy" and "working-class population," for instance) were mere abstractions without a base in real life. The practical consequence of their usage as explanatory factors, whether intended or not, was to hide much more about societal organization than they could ever elucidate.

In bourgeois civil society, everyday productive life appears, on the surface, to be merely egoistic market-oriented individual behaviours. Bourgeois political economy took these socially produced appearances and glorified them as eternal truths (such as "the market" and "supply and demand"). In volume 1 of *Capital* (1867), Marx begins his mature critique of bourgeois political economy and civil society by focusing on the progressive reduction, in capitalist society, of all social values (such as caring) to *commodities*, to things that are produced in order to be bought and sold in a marketplace at their *exchange value*. Thus, individuals *appear* to be freely exchanging what they have for what they "need" based on their individuality.

But, according to Marx's *labour theory of value*, all value is socially produced by human labour power. The exchange value of a commodity is ultimately equivalent to the average amount of labour time socially necessary for its production. Commodities are really just "dead," or previously expended, labour power; they are the "congealed" products of humans' social ability to produce. *Commodity fetishism* is the tendency, in capitalist society, to grant to the thing-for-sale a power over us to define our individuality ("I am Jim; I wear Levis") and to glorify the market as the place where unique personalities can be bought at the same time as a mass-produced commodity. For Marx, commodity fetishism defined both the lack of depth and the limits of bourgeois individualism.

If labour power were in fact the basic source of all commodities, then, Marx reasoned, uncovering the basic social class relationship within the production of these commodities would unveil the real workings of society in a way that commodity fetishists could not attain. This basic class relationship he called *exploitation*.

The hiring of labour by a capitalist enterprise only *appears* to be a free exchange of equivalents in an open labour market between the worker, who agrees to work for a given wage, and the employer, who agrees to pay a certain wage for the labour. In fact, what the capitalist purchases at a certain wage is not the workers' labour but their *labour power*. Because this human capacity to transform the social-material world is the real source of all exchange value, the capitalist in fact purchases the workers' capacity to add value but only pays for what it takes to reproduce the labour involved. What appears to be the purchase of, say, ten hours of work in a given day is actually the purchase of the creative capacity to add value. The worker produces the exchange value equivalent to a daily wage in five hours, for example, and produces new value for the capitalist in the remaining five hours. The extraction of this *surplus value* by the capitalist, above the value of the wage for labour, is the central social class relationship within capitalism, a relationship of the exploitation of the working class by the capitalist class.

In volume 1 of *Capital*, Marx defines the class conflictual aspect of this relationship of exploitation as the class struggle over the *rate of exploitation*, the ratio of surplus value to variable capital (wages), or s/v. From the point of view of capital, the central class contradiction in this social relationship of exploitation is the structural necessity for the capitalist, as capitalist, to attain ever more surplus value from the proletariat. Within capitalism, in order to continue as a capitalist, the capitalist must attempt to raise the rate of exploitation in order to expand; only by increasing the rate of accumulation of surplus value will the capitalist not be driven out of business by other capitalists. Thus, from the point of view of capital, this relationship of exploitation and the tendency for the rate of exploitation to increase are, for Marx, independent of the "good will"—or otherwise—of individual capitalists. Capitalists, to be capitalists, must exploit the working class and must always be developing ways of raising the rate of exploitation.

This structural imperative within capitalism of constantly expanding accumulation by raising the rate of exploitation contains within it the "logic" of all capitals becoming concentrated and centralized into one big capital controlled by the extremely few. Competition among capitalists to increase the rate of exploitation ensures this result.

For Marx, bourgeois or capitalist society was distinguishable from all other hitherto existing class societies by its rapid and ongoing expansion of the mass of privatized wealth (dead labour power) in the hands of increasingly fewer capitalists. At the same time, the everyday life of the proletariat in civil society was being reduced to nothing else, apparently, but economic relations of exchange between individuals who are increasingly "freed" from superstructural constraints, such as laws that required them to supply labour and products for the lords of feudal times, that were unnecessary for expanded capital accumulation. In a word, the vast majority of humanity was being *proletarianized*, "freed" from all obligations except the imperative to survive by selling their labour power.

The very origins of capitalism and its "free labour market" were rooted in transformations that allowed the few to exploit the many. Slavery and colonization provided merchant capital with both a surplus to invest in industry and the raw materials and food to sustain those industries. Much of the peasantry was forcibly cleared off the land in order to provide better rents for wealthy landholders to invest in industry and a landless class that had to work for them or starve. In the towns and cities, the dismantling of the guilds "freed" craftspeople to work in manufacturing industries at low wages and without any of their former rights. "These newly freed men became sellers of themselves only after they had been robbed of all their own means of production, and all the guarantees of existence afforded by the old feudal arrangements. And this history, the history of their expropriation, is written in the annals of mankind in letters of blood and fire."

Within the established organization of capitalism, the structural imperative, for any given capitalist, of increasing the rate of exploitation ensures not only the further proletarianization of the intermediary classes but also the massive *immiseration* of the working class as a whole. The drive to increase the proportion of surplus value relative to wages ensures that an increasing proportion of the working class is driven out of regular work, becoming a *surplus population* and pauperized.

The masses of capital welded together overnight by centralization reproduce and multiply as the others do, only more rapidly, and they thereby become new and powerful levers of social accumulation. Therefore, when we speak of the progress of social accumulation, we tacitly include—these days—the effects of centralization.

The additional capitals formed in the normal course of accumulation serve above all as vehicles for the exploitation of new inventions and discoveries, and industrial improvements in general. But in time the old capital itself reaches the point where it has to be renewed in all its aspects, a time when it sheds its skin and is reborn like the other capitals in a per- fected technical shape, in which a smaller quantity of labour will suffice to set in motion a larger quantity of machinery and raw material. The absolute reduction in the demand for labour which necessarily follows from this is obviously so much the greater, the higher the degree to which the capitals undergoing this process of renewal are already massed togeth- er by virtue of the movement towards centralization.

On the one hand, the additional capital formed in the course of fur- ther accumulation attracts fewer and fewer workers in proportion to its magnitude. On the other hand, the old capital periodically reproduced with a new composition repels more and more of the workers formerly employed by it.

This process of increasing immiseration based on the relative growth of surplus value leads, necessarily, to the growth of an *industrial reserve army* of the unemployed. At any given time, the unemployed are "sur- plus" to the requirements of capital accumulation. Marx termed this process of immiseration and increasing unemployment as the *absolute general law of capital accumulation.* He further identified three fractions of the unemployed: a "floating" segment that regularly goes back and forth between employment and unemployment depending on the economic climate and type of industry; a "latent" segment that is not usually employed but that could be drawn upon in times of capitalist expansion; and a "stagnant" fraction that is left to rot in intolerable conditions of chronic unemployment and degradation.

In volumes 2 and 3 of *Capital* (1885, 1894), both of which Engels compiled from Marx's notes after Marx's death in 1883, Marx contin- ues his critique of political economy *from the point of view of capital,* by examining a whole series of problems inherent in the *realization* of capital in the commodity markets and in the production process. The principal general contradiction within the capital-realization circuit is the long-term tendency towards increasingly severe economic crises due to the overproduction of commodities relative to the declining effective purchasing power of the vast majority. This tendency can be ameliorated, for periods of time, by growth in the production of capital goods for capitalists (machinery, for example) or by growth in con- sumer goods for a segment of the working class that is relatively less impoverished, or by growth in luxury goods for the wealthy.

A much more specific and recurring problem for the capitalist class to resolve stems from the historical tendency for the exchange value of "constant capital" (c, the "dead labour power" of fixed assets used in production such as machinery, raw materials, and the physical plant) to increase relative to "variable capital" (v, wages) as technology displaces living labour power. This relatively steady secular rise in the *organic composition of capital* (c/v) causes a recurring *tendency for the rate of profit to decline*. Basically, as larger and larger portions of surplus value are used to purchase new fixed assets, the rate of profit or return on investment declines.

From the point of view of capital, any lowering of the rate of profit is a crisis indeed—as opposed to the general trend of massive immiseration of the working class! Thus, it is precisely in those recurring periods of a declining rate of profit (such as the early 1970s to the early 1990s) that the largest attacks on the working and living conditions of the working class are organized by the capitalist class and its ideological/superstructural apologists.

There is a great deal more to be learned about Marx's precise critique of the political economy of capitalism. However, even our very brief excursion into the three volumes of *Capital* can allow us to identify two interrelated points within Marx's work that are often seriously misconstrued.

A first point is that all of Marx's law-like statements about the development of contradictions within capitalism are tendential statements. Even Marx's introduction of his absolute general law of capitalist accumulation is immediately followed by the statement, "Like other laws, it is modified in its working by many circumstances, the analysis of which does not concern us here." Such tendential laws were never developed to predict mechanically exactly when, for instance, Armageddon would occur. They were developed as heuristic guides to informed working-class action against the "inner workings" of these only apparently natural exigencies of capital. The principal "circumstances, the analysis of which does not concern us here," were the current conditions and levels of working-class action. For Marx, it was primarily the struggles of the working class to increase the price of its labour power that could slow down, for specific periods, the tendential logic of immiseration. Only the abolition of exploitation through working-class self-emancipation could stop it.

The second interrelated point is that, despite the relentless critique of capital contained therein, all three volumes of *Capital* were in fact, written only from the side of capital, insofar as they examine the structural requisites for "successful" capital accumulation and realization and the tendencies to crisis that occur because of that accumulation and realization. As outlined in *Grundrisse*, Marx's full-fledged critique of political economy was to have included a volume on the critique of capitalism from the side of the working class, focusing on the necessity and possibility of emancipation. Marx died before he could address this issue (and others such as the world market).

The "correct scientific method" that Marx applied to capitalism from the side of capital was never as rigorously worked out from the side of labour in his full-fledged critique of political economy. Nevertheless, while he was developing his critique of political economy, Marx did write thousands of pages of analysis of ongoing class struggles from the side of the working class in which he attempted to discover the social and material bases for societal transformation. It is to these detailed accounts in the so-called Middle Marx that we now turn.

Key Sources

Among the various editions of the works cited in this chapter, see Karl Marx and Frederick Engels's *The Communist Manifesto* (Washington Square, 1964) and Marx's *Grundrisse: Foundations of the Critique of Political Economy* (Penguin, 1973), *A Contribution to the Critique of Political Economy* (Progress, 1970), and *Capital*, 3 vols. (Penguin, 1976, 1977, 1979). *The Communist Manifesto* is probably the most accessible; volume 1 of *Capital* is essential.

Michael Lebowitz's *Beyond Capital: Marx's Political Economy of the Working Class* (Macmillan, 1992) provides an excellent critical overview of Marx's political economy. The introductions to the editions of Marx's work cited above are helpful. If your time is highly limited, read Marx directly.

Suggestions for Research and Debate

1. Discuss commodity fetishism and the purchasing of individuality in current television advertising. To what degree does commodity fetishism rule your daily life?
2. What was gained and what was lost by Marx's focus on exploitation as the expropriation of surplus value from paid, as opposed to unpaid, labour power?
3. If business administration and commerce students were to read Marx, would they be better able to manage capitalism?
4. Has there been a tendency towards immiseration on a world scale during this century? If so, how so? If not, why not?
5. Does the tendency of the rate of profit to decline aid in your understanding of the contemporary level of popular protests? If so, how? If not, what does?
6. Can capitalism be salvaged from its own contradictions? If so, how would it still be capitalism? If not, then why is so much effort spent in doing so?

SIX

Emancipation Ic:
Marx's Theory of Class
Struggles and Societal
Transformation

Karl Marx's theory of human emancipatory potential in his early writing and his later theory of capitalist social organization contained in his critique of political economy were developed primarily in order to inform working-class struggles towards emancipation. In the writings of the so-called Middle Marx, from 1848 until his death, Marx continually tested and revised his developing historical materialist political economy, or social science, in the light of contemporary class struggles and social revolutions.

Marx's careful and committed analyses of a whole series of class struggles, revolutionary and otherwise, drew upon actual working-class collective practice in order to theorize the principal conditions under which, first, capitalist social organization becomes "intolerable" and, second, working class–led revolutionary societal transformation actually becomes possible. As well, the direction of existing revolutionary working-class practices provided Marx with a significant, if necessarily partial, historical materialist understanding of a number of central features of the new society in the making.

The rapid rise and equally rapid military defeat of the armed revolutions of 1848 in western Europe confirmed, for Marx, a number of arguments that he had advanced within the Communist League (1846–52), for which he and Engels had written *The Communist Manifesto*. Marx's stress, shared with Auguste Blanqui, the leader of the organized wing of the French workers' movement, on the overthrow of the existing political state by the organized proletariat was confirmed by the events of the uprisings. However, Blanqui's limitation of the revolution to a merely political revolution was criticized by Marx as undercutting its very possibility of success. For Marx, a full-fledged social (as well as political) revolution was necessary in order to abolish private ownership of the major means of production and create the conditions for the working class's collective control over those means of production. "In place of the old bourgeois society, with its classes and class antagonisms, we shall have an association in which the free development of each is the condition for the free development of all."

Marx's stress on the modern industrial/industrialized working class as the most disciplined, dependable, and resolute core of the proletariat and the central collective subject of revolutionary transformation was also confirmed by actual events. Because of its social concentration in workplaces and thus its ability to combine against the capitalists, the industrial/industrialized working class was more able than other workers to sustain attacks and to push forward a working-class program.

However, in 1848 the modern, industrialized proletariat was simply still too minor a proportion of the European population to lead a successful revolution. The rapid and decisive defeats of the revolutions of 1848 prompted Marx to refute and abandon his own still-idealist notion that clearly written propaganda and timely agitation by a small group of committed workers from a few countries, such as in the Communist League, would be sufficient to overthrow a capitalism seen to be in its "final crisis." The final crisis of capitalism required a much larger and much better-organized industrialized proletariat to enact its transformation. The final crisis was not going to come about by economic crisis alone; it would require massive and massively conscious working-class organization and struggle.

In *The Class Struggles in France* (1848–50) and *The Eighteenth Brumaire of Louis Bonaparte* (1852), Marx applies a historical materialist approach to the situation in France immediately following the attempted revolution of 1848. He addresses the situation where, unlike his and Engels's prediction in *The Communist Manifesto*, the social world had not yet been divided clearly into two class camps, that of the bourgeoisie and the proletariat, and the state therefore had not yet become just "a committee for managing the affairs of the whole bourgeoisie" against the working class.

Given the relative underdevelopment of industrial capitalism in France at the time, Marx portrays a much greater diversity of classes and "fractions" of classes in these works. Fractions of classes—such as the great landowners, the financial bourgeoisie, the industrial bourgeoisie, the petty bourgeoisie with all its gradations, on the one hand, and the industrial proletariat, the *lumpenproletariat* or underclass, and small peasant proprietors, on the other—are painstakingly analysed in terms of the conditions facilitating and hindering their concerted political actions between and among themselves. Louis Bonaparte's successful coup and his subsequent regime are both argued to be the result of the inability of these class fragments to coalesce, as yet, into "two great camps." A ruling bloc led by the "financial aristocracy" had not yet become a capitalist "ruling class" as such. Because of this, Louis Bonaparte could appear to act as if he were beyond and above class considerations. Only with the coalescence of these fractions into more or less two classes would politics be clearly about class domination.

In these two works, as well, Marx analyses the ideological or superstructural representations of class interests that were peculiar to each class fraction, and to which specific ideologists attached themselves, and he demonstrates their power as a social-political force in the world. Unlike the many later mechanistic Marxists who memorize a part of Marx's theory, such as the two-class model and base-superstructure paradigm, in order to reduce social reality to that part that has been memorized, Marx's analysis gives precedence to actual practice. Far from being a forced, mechanistic application of a complete and completed theoretical framework "from above" onto concrete class practices, *The Class Struggles in France* and *The Eighteenth Brumaire of Louis Bonaparte* are superb exemplars of Marx's application of historical materialism in which the actual story of practice takes precedence over, informs, and thereby enriches the material historicity of the theory.

43

The defeats of the revolutions of 1848 taught Marx that his critique of political economy had to be deepened; this he did in the works discussed in the preceding chapter of this text. More to the point here, Marx learned that only the longer-term, more gradual building up of a truly extensive international organization of leading workers and their national organizations, centred on the rapidly expanding industrialized proletariat and steeled in the social science of historical materialism, could actually make possible a self-emancipatory working-class state. Thus, when the International Working Men's Association (later referred to as the First International, 1864–76) was founded, Marx brought to it not only a much more incisive critique of capitalist political economy but also a renewed commitment to guide the majority of its various reformist sections to a revolutionary program. This program was to be based upon the social science of historical materialism and on the abiding anti-elitist principle, first clearly enunciated by Marx and Engels in *The Communist Manifesto* (1848), of the *self-emancipation of the working class*: the "emancipation of the working class must be the act of the working class itself"; "the first step in the revolution by the working class is to raise the proletariat to the position of the ruling class, to win the battle of democracy."

Among the elitist reformisms Marx criticized in the 1860s and early 1870s were the French Proudhonists' and English Owennites' utopian socialist programs of co-operatively owned and controlled capitalist enterprises, and German Social Democracy's opportunistic and economistic tendency to make only strictly economic, defensive demands. Indeed, in the first draft of *The Civil War in France*, Marx even criticized a tiny section of the International for its "Comtism": "Comte is known to the Parisian workmen as the prophet in politics of Imperialism (of personal *dictatorship*), of capitalist rule in political economy, of hierarchy in all spheres of human action, even in the sphere of science, and as the author of a new catechism with a new pope and new saints in place of the old ones."

In the spring of 1871, the working class and its allies established the Paris Commune after seizing control of Paris and a number of other cities in France following the humiliating defeat of the French army by Prussian forces at the very gates of Paris. Within two months, the Commune's brief flowering had been violently suppressed by the combined military might of the Prussian and French forces. This first-ever experience of working-class state power, and its subsequent defeat, provided Marx with numerous practical—and tactical—lessons. These lessons included the importance of the working class retaining its arms and its vigilance against class enemies until they were thoroughly defeated ("the dictatorship of the proletariat"), of seizing collective control of all major bourgeois private property such as the banks, and of not just taking over the bureaucracy but transforming it into a much more democratic form.

The strategic lessons drawn from the actual positive experiences of the working class–led self-organization of the Paris Commune made the most valuable contribution to Marx's understanding of what self-emancipating working-class rule actually encompassed. For Marx, the "true secret" of the Paris Commune was:

> It was essentially a working-class government, the product of the struggle of the producing against the appropriating classes, the political form at last discovered under which to work out the economical emancipation of labour.... By the constitution of the Commune, they have taken the actual management of their revolution into their own hands and found at the same time, in the case of success, the means to hold it in the hands of the people itself, displacing the machinery of the ruling classes by a governmental machinery of their own.

In many of the Commune's actions—such as the abolition of the standing army, the vesting of political power in delegates who were subject to recall, the standardization of delegates' pay to the average proletarian wage, the working (executive, legislative, and judicial) unity of the Commune, and the generalization of the Commune form to every level of government—Marx saw the living possibility of actual popular power (*demos kratos*, the people rule). These actions had extended beyond the mere mouthing of "liberty, equality, and solidarity" in bourgeois minority-class rule to become the actual practice of all in the very process of the suppression of exploitation and class rule in general.

Socialist democracy through working-class self-rule could actually occur and would, Marx asserted, eventually create a classless global humanity of communism, the end of systematic oppression in all forms, and the beginning of unalienated existence. For Marx, so-called anti-authoritarian-conspiracy organizers, like the anarchist-communist Bakunin, who would immediately "smash the state" before the conditions of classlessness had been created, were not only hopelessly utopian but also profoundly anti-democratic in both their short-term practices and the longer-term consequences. Rather, the growth in industrial capitalism, and thus of the industrial proletariat, was opening up real possibilities for the working class not only to unionize but to form itself into mass political parties in each state in which parliamentary opposition was allowable.

For Marx as well as Engels, organizing mass working-class parties, where applicable, became a priority in the advancement of a working-class revolutionary program. However, in his *Critique of the Gotha Programme* (1875) of the German Social Democratic Party and elsewhere during this time period, Marx argued that these newly emergent mass working-class parties must attract allies through their parliamentary struggles; maintain an internationalist outlook and never give in to narrow nationalist concerns; prepare themselves for the principal goal of state power by the working class; understand that a "peaceful road" to socialism was not likely to be a normal route to state power because of the preponderance in almost all bourgeois states of bureaucratic-military state power that would likely require force to defeat and transform; and constantly beware of the influx of proponents of bourgeois and petty bourgeois ideologies into the leaderships of the parties.

Marx's Marxism was consistently rooted in class analysis and class struggles; its main point was to explain the class conditions that limited the free development of human potential in order to eradicate the class-rooted systematic bases for those limitations. It was assumed by Marx that eradicating *class* conditions of exploitation through self-emancipatory class struggles would greatly facilitate the elimination of other forms of systematized oppression, such as by "race," gender, and age.

After Marx's death, Frederick Engels (1820–95) developed this argument in his still controversial *The Origin of the Family, Private Property, and the State* (1884). Engels argues that working-class self-emancipation requires and facilitates the elimination of other forms of systematic oppression such as sexism and racism. Without the end of the exploitation of the majority classes by the minority class, sexism and racism can, he argued, never be systematically eliminated. In all pre-socialist

45

societies, the minority ruling class requires such structured inequalities to divide and rule the majority classes. Only socialist and communist societies, he reckoned, could be committed to uniting humanity. Clearly, much remains to be developed within Marxism concerning the adequate analysis of the specific ways in which domestic and human reproductive labour power is usurped mostly by men at the expense of women.

A few of the other self-authored writings of the elderly Engels have proven to be even more controversial within Marxism. In some places, Engels seems to conflate natural and biological science with historical materialism and to present Marxism as basically a purely objective science of a supra-historical set of determinations that are said to be rooted in the social evolution of the forces of production. To the extent that this is true, Marx's Marxism is changed from historical materialism, which stresses creative, "subjective" practice under specific "objective" conditions that are independent of one's own consciousness, to a merely predetermined dialectical unfolding of objective laws that are completely independent of human creative practice.

As we have seen, Marx's Marxism is two-sided, both objective and subjective. For Marx, totally subjective freedom does not exist in any known society. By the same token, the totally objective determination of human practice does not exist even in capitalist class society. For Marx, the real dance is the partnership of the objective and the subjective in the making of transformative social change through informed and collective self-emancipatory practice under conditions both of necessity and of possibility. For Marx, again, the point is not just to interpret the social world; the point is to change it through collective action.

Key Sources

Three sources of Marx's writings contain all of the material referred to in this chapter: *The Revolutions of 1848* (Penguin, 1973), *Surveys from Exile* (Penguin, 1973), and *The First International and After* (Penguin, 1974). If you have already read *The Communist Manifesto*, which is in the first book, try *The Civil War in France* contained in the third.

Dongno Kim's "The Theoretical Foundation of Marx's Historical Sociology," *Critical Sociology* 21, 1 (1995): 81–100, provides an excellent brief overview of Marx's entire Marxism. Joseph Ferraro's *Freedom and Determination in History According to Marx and Engels* (Monthly Review Press, 1992) argues for Marx's dialectical unity of both freedom and determination. S.H. Rigby's *Engels and the Formation of Marxism* (Manchester University Press, 1992) gives a relatively measured assessment of Engels's contributions to Marxism.

Suggestions for Research and Debate

1. To what degree are the conditions that make capitalism intolerable to the working class also the conditions that make socialism possible?

2. What, if any, are the conditions that make capitalism intolerable to the working class today?

3. What, if any, are the conditions that make socialism possible today?

4. Why was it so important to Marx's Marxism to explain the dialectical unity of human freedom and determination, or subjectivity and objectivity? Is it still important to adequate social theorizing?

5. Is it possible to have a classless analysis of gender or of race that is also emancipatory for the great majority of humans? Why or why not?

6. When Marx realized how many people were misinterpreting his theory in mechanistic-determinist or reformist ways he claimed that he was, therefore, not a Marxist! What are the historical-material social bases that have facilitated others to so often reduce Marx's Marxism to mere determinism or reformism?

47

Elite Engineering II: Herbert Spencer's "Radicalism," Social Evolutionism, and Constraint Engineering

48

Like Marx's theory, the social theorizing of Herbert Spencer (1820–1903) synthesized important aspects of both an Enlightened viewpoint and the prevailing scientific insights, such as they were, of the nineteenth century. Unlike Marx, however, Spencer never critically evaluated the bourgeois, ideological roots of the Enlightenment viewpoint. Instead of critiquing, as best he could, the prevailing science and social reality, Spencer steadfastly developed a full-fledged social theoretical justification for unrestricted capitalism. After a half century of being scorned as reactionary "Social Darwinism," Spencer's theory has re-emerged as the social theoretical basis for institutionalized neo-liberal ideological dominance.

Spencer was born in Derby, England, of a Methodist mother and a father who was a self-employed school teacher. His secondary education was almost entirely in the mechanical-instrumental natural sciences. Devoid as he was of any contamination from the humanities, Spencer became a civil engineer at the age of sixteen, never attending university. He was to become one of the most popular "gentlemen amateurs" of his times, one whose presence was much in demand at the estates of the English upper class and whose writings were, in the late nineteenth century, regularly required reading in major biology, psychology, and sociology departments in both England and the United States.

Throughout his life, Spencer steadfastly maintained a particular version of the Enlightenment viewpoint known as middle-class radicalism, which he had first imbibed from his father and from the emergent class of shopkeepers and small-scale manufacturers in the still relatively rural setting of his youth and which had already been constituted as the dominant ideology in the United States. This middle-class radicalism was profoundly anti-aristocratic and anti-militaristic, and advocated the strict separation of church and state. In these ways, it was, like the

Enlightenment, a "radical" critique of the remaining elements of what was now seen to be a feudal past.

Like the Enlightenment, as well, *middle-class radicalism* strongly believed in human reason as a guide to social progress through the gradual attainment of what were assumed to be "the natural rights of man." In common with most Enlightenment theory, middle-class radicalism stressed the individualistic aspects of these "natural rights." Such radicalism proclaimed equality of opportunity for each and all, but justified inequalities of condition (such as class and "racial" inequalities) as necessary, rooted as they were in the sacredness of privatized property. As such, middle-class radicalism was not socially radical at all.

The absolute reduction of natural rights to individualistic, *not* social, rights was most clearly and consistently expressed in middle-class radicalism's vehement attacks on the persistence and growth of state regulatory authority and, even more so, on the emerging demon of "collectivism" as expressed in the unionism and socialism of the popular classes and in popular uprisings in the colonies. In these respects, middle-class radicalism was (and still is) deeply socially reactionary.

Herbert Spencer's social theory was developed explicitly to provide this increasingly reactionary radicalism with an apparently scientific set of justifications for individualism in order to confront the twin demons of government regulation and popular-class collectivism. That this was consciously Spencer's project is evidenced in his earliest treatise, *Social Statics: or, the Conditions Essential to Human Happiness Specified* (1851), and in one of his later works, *The Man versus the State* (1884). Both works are ethical diatribes against the state's interfering to level, to any extent, conditions of social inequality. Both advocate the importance of individual development through disciplined self-effort and "pulling oneself up by one's own bootstraps" as the only true source of happiness. Both attack collectivist approaches to human development as guaranteed to produce human unhappiness and, at any rate, as doomed to failure. Only laissez-faire ("leave us alone!") capitalism, which permitted individuals to profit as they saw fit, would allow human happiness and further societal progress.

To bolster these diatribes, Spencer's major life-project was the development of his *synthetic philosophy*. The scholarly goal of this philosophy was to discover the fundamental, uniform, and causal principles that supposedly unified all the sciences and ethics. Much of his voluminous written work is an attempt to show, in considerable detail, how these basic principles operated in each of the fields of biology, psychology, sociology, and ethics.

In *First Principles* (1862), Spencer differentiated between the scientifically "knowable" and the scientifically "unknowable," or "ultimate,"

49

reality. In a uniformly reductionist and *positivist* fashion, then, Spencer discarded the pursuit of what was currently unknowable by existing science as a "worthless" enterprise. On the basis of what he saw as a universal process of change in all matter, Spencer posited a set of uniform, naturalistic, and causal "first principles," derived from the mechanical physics and biology of his time. By means of these principles, it was held that one could attain certain knowledge of the rules facilitating the "evolution" or "dissolution" of all matter, including social "matter." This *naturalistic-evolutionist* paradigm of causal rules for all matter was argued to consist of the interrelated processes of generally progressive increases in mass, density, differentiation, specialization, integration, and adaptation.

Unlike Comte's positivism, Spencer was careful not to arrange the sciences in a hierarchy topped by sociology. Instead, his tendency was to reduce all science, including social science, to what he saw to be universal and uniform principles of change, of evolution and dissolution, that could be applied, with some variation, to what he termed the three forms of material reality: the physical, the organic, and the *superorganic* or societal.

In both his early essay "The Social Organism" (1860) and in his three volumes of *The Principles of Sociology* (1876–96), Spencer followed the tradition that Auguste Comte had helped to reintroduce from the classical Greeks and Romans—that of treating societies as if they were living organisms. However, unlike Comte before him and Emile Durkheim and many others after him, Herbert Spencer was careful to identify not just the uniformities between societies and organisms but also "a cardinal difference."

> Hence, then, a cardinal difference in the two kinds of organisms. In the one case [the biological organism], consciousness is concentrated in a small part of the aggregate. In the other [the social organism], it is diffused throughout the aggregate: all the units possess the capacities for happiness and misery, if not in equal degress, still in degress that approximate. As, then, there is no social sensorium, the welfare of the aggregate, considered apart from that of the units, is not an end to be sought. The society exists for the benefit of its members; not its members for the benefit of society. It has ever to be remembered that great as may be the efforts made for the prosperity of the body politic, yet the claims of the body politic are nothing in themselves, and become something only in so far as they embody the claims of its component individuals.
>
> From this last consideration, which is a digression rather than a part of the argument, let us now return and sum up the reasons for regarding society as an organism.
>
> It undergoes continuous growth. As it grows, its parts become unlike:

it exhibits increase of structure. The unlike parts simultaneously assume activities of unlike kinds. These activities are not simply different, but their differences are so related as to make one another possible. The reciprocal aid thus given causes mutual dependence of the parts. And the mutually dependent parts, living by and for one another, form an aggregate constituted on the same general principle as is an individual organism. The analogy of a society to an organism becomes still clearer on learning that every organism of appreciable size is a society; and on further learning that in both, the lives of the units continue for some time if the life of the aggregate is suddenly arrested, while if the aggregate is not destroyed by violence, its life greatly exceeds the duration of the lives of its units. Though the two are contrasted as respectively discrete and concrete and though there results a difference in the ends subserved by the organization, there does not result a difference in the laws of the organization: the required mutual influences of the parts, not transmissible in a direct way, being, in a society, transmitted in an indirect way.

51

Like other organisms, the "social organism" or human society slowly grows in "mass" or size and in structural complexity, and the parts become increasingly mutually dependent and functionally integrated. In both biological and social organisms, the whole lives longer than its individual parts. However, Spencer argued that, in contrast to biological organisms, societies do not have a fixed and readily observable form, and the units or individuals may be physically dispersed and without direct contact and are highly mobile. Most important, for Spencer, within societies consciousness is not centralized in one component part; each individual part is capable of independent consciousness of reality, subject only to the given level of societal development.

To return to the terms we have used to evaluate other theorists discussed in this volume, Figure 7.1 illustrates that Spencer viewed human beings as capable of conscious reasoning, choosing, and acting, but only at the given level of societal advancement. Indeed, Spencer's entire *social evolutionist* theory is informed with a notion of human beings as perfectible *within* the gradual, evolutionary development of the social organism—human society—towards perfection. Spencer was positive about *both* the progressive evolution of human beings and of society; the evolution of the individual and of society were correlated and viewed as interdependent.

Developed in the same social milieu and during the same period in which Charles Darwin wrote, Spencer's social theory was concerned not so much with the origin of the species as with the causal determination of the evolutionary stages of the superorganic life of the social organism. In *The Principles of Sociology*, he lists five such stages, which he placed in a hierarchy determined "scientifically" by the naturalist-evo-

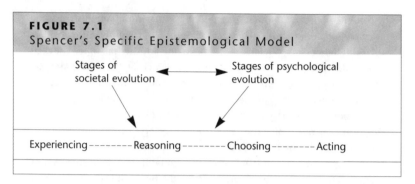

FIGURE 7.1
Spencer's Specific Epistemological Model

Stages of societal evolution ⟷ Stages of psychological evolution

Experiencing -------- Reasoning -------- Choosing -------- Acting

lutionist "first principles" of increasing size, density, differentiation, specialization, integration, and adaptation. He focused primarily on the three structural-functional processes within a given stage of society: the "operative," "sustaining," or "internal" productive function; the "regulatory" or "external" function; and the "distributive" or communication function. These five stages were said to be: the simple without leadership; the simple with leadership; the compound; the doubly compound; and the trebly compound.

Additionally, each of the more "advanced" stages of societal evolution could be distinguished by whether it was more inclined to the militant or the industrial form. Militant societies were dominated by the "regulatory" function and tended towards state domination of the individual; industrial societies were dominated by the "sustaining," productive function and tended to enhance individual freedom. For Spencer, the height of societal evolution thus far was the trebly compound industrial society to which England was approaching, if only it could rid itself of its nobility and other feudal "survivals" and its penchant for state regulation and tolerance for collectivism.

When compared to other social evolutionist theories being developed in the same period by British anthropologists, Spencer's terms for the hierarchical and categorical stages seem somewhat less ethnocentric than the usual hierarchical trilogy of "savage" or "primitive," "barbarian," and "civilized" so fashionable in the expansion of the British Empire and so self-justificatory of imperialist conquest. Nevertheless, despite his less overtly racist terminology and his disdain for militarism, Spencer's social evolutionist theory is at least as invidious as those of his contemporaries.

As in British anthropology of the time, Spencer's hierarchy was a theoretical justification for the subordination and even "dissolution" of societies and peoples in a "lower" stage by societies in a "higher" stage. Because higher-stage societies were more integrated and adaptable than lower-stage societies, they would "naturally" outlive the lesser kinds. In common with evolutionist anthropologists, Spencer viewed contemporary simple societies, judged through the ethnographic reports of various Christian missionaries, as anachronistic survivals from a much earlier era; they were doomed to extinction by the iron laws of naturalistic evolution.

Spencer's equally positive and positivist view of both human potential and societal evolution allowed him to conflate his views on psychological and sociological evolution in particularly ageist ways. Spencer viewed the evolution of societies from simple to trebly compound as almost exactly akin to an individual's maturation or personal "evolution." Simple societies were like infants, which would either grow up, aided, ideally, by the example of more advanced adults, or not evolve and therefore die off. Thus, for Spencer, both societies and individuals tended to "evolve" towards the highest developmental stages or be trapped at a given stage and die off. The fact that in Spencer's categorization, only non-white societies populated the lower stages of societal evolution, and that only some white societies were approaching the apex of trebly compound industrialism, was taken to be the naturalistic, evolutionary proof of the necessity of racial inequalities.

Women, as well, were argued to be necessarily stunted in their personal evolution, within whatever stage of societal development, because their reproductive duty in all societies kept them from growing up to become fully developed "men." The laws of naturalistic evolution, according to Spencer, forbade the highest stage of maturity or development to women. Thus "the white man's burden" was manifold: to advance for themselves in order to give some guidance, no matter how unrequited, to the young, the female, the non-white, the simple.

Spencer's correlated psychology and sociology were firmly rooted in Lamarckian evolutionary principles that stressed that both biological and psychological traits developed through use and decayed through disuse and that those that had been regularly used by individuals would be transmitted on to the next biological generation. The assumption of these principles allowed Spencer to posit the gradual, intergenerational transfer of rational-cognitive abilities and, even more important, irrational-emotional "sentiments" appropriate to the given societal stage. These Lamarckian assumptions were crucial to Spencer's positing "scientifically" the ultimate advance of society, based on the development of those who best adapted to their social environment and most exercised their abilities. In this context, Herbert Spencer, not Charles Darwin, coined the phrase *the survival of the fittest* as an iron law of naturalistic evolution linking the individual to the social organism. The best-adapted will, naturally, best survive and pass on their superior traits to their biological progeny. In the short term of individual lives, the rest be damned. Any attempt to prolong the survival of less-adapt-

53

TABLE 7.1
Spencer's Stance on Humans, Existing Societal Organization, and the Possibility of Radical Social Change

Human potential	Highly positive view of potential for individual freedom, especially for white men in advanced societies (High + for some; high − for most)
Existing societal organization	Highly positive, in the long run of societal evolution (High +)
Possibility of radical social change	Impossible according to the laws of societal evolution—only gradual, cumulative alterations possible (High −)

ed individuals would only be retrogressive for humanity as a whole in the very long term of societal and psychological evolution.

Spencer's survival of the fittest implies, of course, the tautology that the winners (for instance, the wealthy) are the evolutionary fittest because they exercised the most appropriate abilities and that they are fittest because they are the winners. This has been a principal catch phrase of liberal capitalism, with its emphasis on free trade and freedom to exploit, and its apologists ever since. Its converse, that losers deserve to lose and should not be supported in any way for the long-term good of both society and humanity, provides crucial "scientific" justification for "blaming the victim" ideologies.

Obviously, for Spencer, the causal rules of naturalistic, gradual evolution made radical societal change of existing advanced societies neither necessary nor possible. What was both necessary and possible to change within the evolution of advanced society, in order to facilitate the quicker fulfilment of these causal rules, was the diminishing of the state's regulatory "function" to only those tasks required for military defence and the guarantee of individual natural rights. In particular, the state's provision of any kind of social rights, such as the regulation of working hours and the right not to starve, had to be forever eliminated. Such collectivist regulations could only retard the necessary advance of society towards industrialism through free competition and the psychological evolution of individuals towards freedom through self-improvement.

As summarized in Table 7.1, Spencer's value-stance (−/+ + −) varied slightly from the Comtean and, as we shall see, the normal elite engi-neering stance in social theory (– + –) in so far as some individuals, especially white men in "advanced" societies, were deemed to have extremely high human potential. Like the normal elite engineering approach, the vast majority of humanity was, however, doomed to remain lower than the elite.

Spencer called upon those who were most advanced or best adapted to become active social engineers in designing and leading the cutback of state collective services. This was, it was argued, for the good of society as a whole even if it were not seen to be so by the majorities who were negatively affected by the cuts. For Spencer, elite-led cuts in the regulatory state would quicken the "natural" development of completely laissez-faire capitalism, the highest stage of societal and personal development that Spencer could envision.

Thus, unlike Comte before him and Durkheim after him, who both called for the expansion of social services managed by an elite corps of social engineers that they had trained, Spencer's theory implies a social elite who consciously practises the *social engineering of restraint*. The plethora of neo-liberal, "scientific" technocrats that manage so many corporations and state institutions in our contemporary world, including an increasing number of our universities, are, wittingly or unwittingly, contemporary expressions of the nineteenth-century Spencerian "science" of the survival of the fittest and of blaming the victim through the advancement of laissez-faire capitalism.

Key Sources

Two of Herbert Spencer's ethical diatribes are in *Social Statics* and *The Man versus the State* (D. Appleton, 1897). "The Social Organism" is included in J.D.Y. Peel's edition of *Herbert Spencer on Social Evolution* (University of Chicago Press, 1972). Two of Spencer's larger works are *First Principles* (P.F. Collier and Son, 1902) and *The Principles of Sociology* (D. Appleton, 1898).

J.D.Y. Peel's *Herbert Spencer: The Evolution of a Sociologist* (Basic Books, 1971) and David Wilshire's *The Social and Political Thought of Herbert Spencer* (Oxford University Press, 1978) give contrasting accounts of Spencer's life and thought, while Marvin Harris's *The Rise of Anthropological Theory* (Thomas Y. Crowell, 1968) and George W. Stocking, Jr's *Victorian Anthropology* (Free Press, 1987) provide contrast-ing accounts of the intellectual environment.

A positivist antidote to my generally negative treatment of Spencer's theory is Jonathan H. Turner, *Herbert Spencer: A Renewed Appreciation* (Sage, 1985).

Suggestions for Research and Debate

1. Compare (and contrast) Comte's and Spencer's structuralism and use of the organismic analogy. What are the deficiencies in each?
2. How does Spencer's social evolutionism deny the history and current validity of radical societal change and of radical personal change?
3. Is social evolutionism necessarily racist? Sexist? Ageist? Why or why not?
4. What are important similarities between the social engineering of expansion and the social engineering of restraint? Which form of social engineering is more elitist? Why?
5. Identify a manager or management team in an institution near you that exhibits social engineering by restraint. To what degree does Spencer's theory underlie the justifications for the restraint?

Elite Engineering III: Emile Durkheim's Positivist and Structuralist Corporatism and the Problem of Socialization

EIGHT

Born in Epinal in the province of Lorraine, France, into a locally influential Jewish family, (David) Emile Durkheim (1858–1917) ended an eight-generation-long line of rabbis in the family by becoming an agnostic. He devoted his entire life to pursuing his "moral calling" of defining and institutionalizing the legitimacy of sociology as a separate and socially necessary academic discipline. Very much like Auguste Comte before him, Durkheim's calling was motivated, throughout his academic life, by what he saw as the moral anarchy or disunity of modern society, especially in France.

The defeat of that country in the Franco-Prussian War, the rise and extermination of the Paris Commune, the continual political intrigues and crises, and the spread of seemingly unsolvable class conflicts in industry were all evidence of such moral anarchy in France. These events confirmed for Durkheim that his "duty" to France and to modern society in general was to found a social science capable of explaining *and* reorganizing or reforming modern society to alleviate the moral "disorganization" and individualistic "decadence" he saw around him.

As an undergraduate in philosophy and history, Durkheim read Saint-Simon, Comte, and Spencer in his spare time. Upon receiving a doctorate from the University of Paris, Durkheim pursued a career in the Faculty of Education at the University of Bordeaux, where he introduced a sociology course into the curriculum and held the Chair of Social Science. In 1902, he accepted the Chair of the Science of Education at the prestigious Sorbonne in Paris, and in 1913, that post was changed to the Chair of the Science of Education and Sociology.

By all accounts, Emile Durkheim was an inspiring professor of his particular social theory to large numbers of graduate students who went on, in a variety of social scientific disciplines, to spread his theoretical approach. A prolific writer whose works were highly acclaimed both by academics and state bureaucrats who shared his republican social reformism, Durkheim also founded the first sociology research institute in the world and co-organized and edited one of the most influential academic journals in sociology. He is often considered, along with Karl Marx and Max Weber, one of the "Big Three" in classical sociological theory.

In terms of social theory, however, much of Durkheim's foundational theorization of what he saw to be the increasingly threatening societal problem of moral anarchy or moral disintegration, was a reformulation, or professionalization, if you will, of the work of the earlier social engineers we have already introduced in this text. As we will see, Durkheim's theoretical solution to modern society's central problem drew from and recombined into a more socially and academically acceptable package a number of central ideas from Saint-Simon, Bonald, de Maistre, Comte, and Spencer. Indeed, it would not be too oversimplified to view Durkheim's theoretical project as a somewhat more liberal and substantially more modern, secular, and rigorous version of Auguste Comte's sociology.

In his first major work, *The Division of Labour in Society* (1893), Durkheim adopted Saint-Simon's stress on the distinctive nature of industrial society with its high division of labour relative to all previous societies. Like Comte, Durkheim's main concern was to discover the moral glue appropriate to create, maintain, and enhance *social solidarity* in newly emergent industrial society. Using many of Spencer's principles of social evolution, he attempted to discover and explain the evolutionary development of the "moral facts" that distinguish industrial society from all others.

Principal among these facts was the evolutionary change away from simple *mechanical solidarity* based on similarity in activity, a shared world-view, almost no modern sense of individuality, and, thus, a very high degree of positive identification with the society as a whole. With the social evolution to industrial society, mechanical solidarity necessarily changed to a much more complex and dynamic *organic solidarity* based on an increasing multiplicity of separated activities, diversification of world-views, an increasing degree of self-centred individualism, and, thus, a real tendency to a low degree of positive identification with society as a whole.

In *The Division of Labour in Society* Durkheim resolved the "problem" of growing individualism and declining identification with society as a whole by means of the old organismic, functionalist analogy of Bonald and de Maistre as developed by Comte and Spencer, among others. With increasing occupational specialization, he argued, came increased *functional dependence* between the individuals and groups that resulted from that greater division of labour. This functional dependence was the structural basis for the potential integration, or "normal" well-being of society.

Indeed, from *The Division of Labour in Society* onward, Durkheim extended Spencer's notion of the "social organism" to its physiological, *corporatist* extreme. He treated society as a normally well, living body, with its normally well-integrated institutions, groups, and individuals functioning as organs. He "diagnosed" many problems within that societal body as "symptoms" of "abnormal" aberrations, "illnesses," or "pathologies," which needed to be "cured" in order for the societal patient to be brought back to normal health. Curing such social pathologies, no matter how bothersome, would facilitate continued societal well-being or health.

For Durkheim, a major pathology arising within the normally well-integrated "organic" division of labour was the high degree of class conflict apparent throughout France and much of the rest of Europe at the time. Unlike Marx, who argued that class conflict was integral to industrial capitalist society, Durkheim argued that such conflicts neither were inherent to the societal body nor should they be seen as signs of terminal illness. Instead, both the *anomic* features of the division of labour, in which normative standards of healthy conduct were weak or absent, and the *forced* features caused by inequalities in the social distribution of wealth were mere abnormalities. These could be cured by the formulation of clear and just, *restitutive*, as opposed to *coercive*, laws and other rules—definitely not by radically transforming the body through revolution.

On the other hand, criminal behaviour and other "deviations" from existing norms were, for Durkheim, mainly seen as not pathological for the societal body. Instead, they were solid indicators of societal well-being insofar as "deviant" behaviour and its treatment in society actually function to clarify the real boundaries of existing norms and normal behaviour. All organic societies need crime and other deviance in order to make visible and clear what the societal system's constraints actually are.

Throughout his work, Durkheim regularly collapsed three separate meanings of "normal" into his theorization: the normal as normative, that is, as rule-guided or norm-following; the normal as statistically average (modal, mean, and median); and the normal as being well, not ill. This word-trick allowed Durkheim to argue that the normative was (or at least should be) the usual and was a sign of societal, institutional, group, and individual good health. Abnormality meant failing to follow the rules, deviating from the statistical mean, median, or mode, and being sick.

The Division of Labour in Society introduced Durkheim's structuralist corporatism not only in the sense of his medical-analytic view of society as a normally well-integrated body: it also introduced his structuralist corporatism as a curative solution to, or treatment for, societal illnesses or problems. In opposition to Comte, who positively assigned the societal regulatory function to the state alone (albeit *his* positive state), Durkheim followed Saint-Simon, to an extent, in calling for the reform of society based on reinstituting, in modern form, the *occupational corporations* or "guilds" that had flourished among the artisans of feudal times. Contrary to Spencer, Durkheim did not advocate "freeing" the "sustaining" or productive capitalist sector of society from most of the regulative control of the state. Rather, he proposed, in increasing detail throughout his scholarly life, a corporatist plan in which the various social classes in a given industry would form across-class corporations that would gradually assume the regulatory functions of the state at the local, regional, and national levels of the body politic.

The Rules of Sociological Method (1895) provides a clear outline of Durkheim's positivist and structural-realist metatheoretical approach to the adequate explanation of societal problems of cohesion and of orderly, evolutionary change. Here, Durkheim adopted and further "scientized" the Comtean triple meaning of positivism—*positing* or developing testable lawful propositions in order to attain *certainty* in explanation and prediction in order to make society *even better*.

For Durkheim as for Comte, society was the most complex *"sui generis"* reality, inexplicable by other, less complex realities, such as those explained by biology and psychology. While evolving from lower level "facts," *social facts*, including moral facts, were seen as entirely distinct from, and actively constitutive of, societal reality. Indeed, "general social facts" were seen as *external* to and *constraining* upon the institutional, group, and even the individual-interactive sublevels of societal reality. "Society is not the mere sum of individuals, but the system formed by their association represents a specific reality which has its own characteristics."

> Here, then, is a category of facts with very distinctive characteristics: it consists of ways of acting, thinking, and feeling, external to the individual, and endowed with a power of coercion, by reason of which they control him. These ways of thinking could not be confused with biological phenomena, since they consist of representations and of actions; nor with psychological phenomena, which exist only in the individual consciousness and through it. They constitute, thus, a new variety of phenomena; and it is to them exclusively that the term "social" ought to be applied. And this term fits them quite well, for it is clear that, since their source is not in the individual, their substratum can be no other than society, either the political society as a whole or some one of the partial groups it includes, such as religious denominations, political, literary, and occupa-

tional associations, etc. On the other hand, this term "social" applies to them exclusively, for it has a distinct meaning only if it designates exclusively the phenomena which are not included in any of the categories of facts that have already been established and classified. These ways of thinking and acting therefore constitute the proper domain of sociology. It is true that, when we define them with this word "constraint," we risk shocking the zealous partisans of absolute individualism. For those who profess the complete autonomy of the individual, man's dignity is diminished whenever he is made to feel that he is not completely self-determinant. It is generally accepted today, however, that most of our ideas and our tendencies are not developed by ourselves but come to us from without. How can they become a part of us except by imposing themselves upon us? This is the whole meaning of our definition. And it is generally accepted, moreover, that social constraint is not necessarily incompatible with the individual personality.

Throughout his scholarly life, Durkheim maintained what he himself called the *dualism of human nature* in industrial or organic society. On the one hand, modern individuals in their isolation and egoism (what Marx called alienation) were capable of producing only socially unshared and thus socially unimportant *individual representations*. On the other hand, socially shared and thus socially important thoughts, feelings, values, norms, and expressive symbols, or *collective representations*, were the product of the societal *conscience collective*, an active and relatively unified collective consciousness and moral conscience that guided and constrained individual, group, and institutional actions.

Durkheim's *Rules of Sociological Method* argues that the *conscience collective* generally and externally constrains individual thinking, feeling, choosing, and acting and, thereby, provides the glue to hold society together. Instead of probing, like Marx had done, the concrete structural conditions that underpinned the apparent dualism in humanity, Durkheim assumed this dualism to be a natural condition of social evolution. Thus, Durkheim's structural realism made active and reified—or made into a thing with self-contained human qualities—society, social facts, and the *conscience collective*. Durkheim's social theory and sociology were concerned with individual experiences, reasonings and feelings, choices and actions, only insofar as they were constrained by an external and generalized societal consciousness and morality.

Suicide: A Study in Sociology (1897) is Durkheim's most famous positivist examination of one "social indicator" of societal illness: the comparative extent to which individuals in differing societies and social groupings kill themselves. While this study has been much cited in methodology courses as an early exemplar of the application of a positivist methodology stressing "objective" and demonstrably "measurable"

FIGURE 8.1
Durkheim's Structural-Realist Epistemological Model

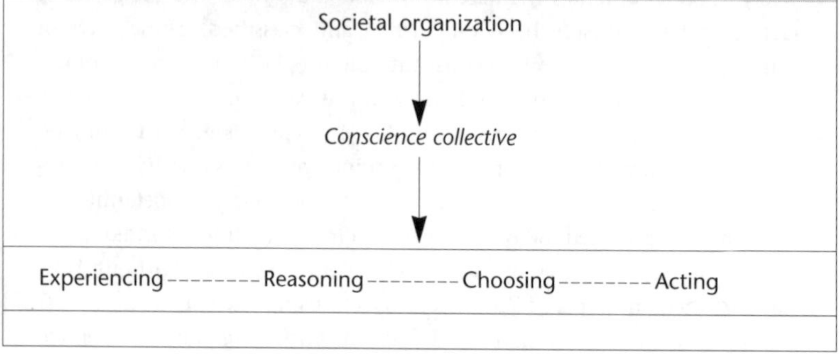

Societal organization

↓

Conscience collective

↓

Experiencing --------- Reasoning --------- Choosing --------- Acting

---

lawful relationships among social facts, the theoretical point to be made here is Durkheim's lack of even a positivist concern for "individual representations" in *Suicide*. His failure, for instance, to ask persons who have attempted suicide why they might have done so, like his prior failure to ask "deviants" why they deviated, is accounted for not by his methodological positivism but by his structuralist corporatism.

Durkheim did not view suicide as both a social and individual problem. Rather, he treated it as strictly a social indicator of the type and degree of "maladjustments" in the societal body such that the rate of suicide "varies inversely" with the degree of societal "integration." Durkheim argued that "altruistic" suicide, or dying for one's country, was caused by too strong a degree of social integration, such as was most common in "lower," mechanical societies but also apparent in modern wars. Much more typical of maladjustments, especially in the period of transition from mechanical to organic societies, were "egoistic" suicides, caused by too low a level of personal integration into society, and "anomic" suicides, caused by the absence or weakness of clear socio-moral rules governing society. These latter two types of suicide could be greatly lessened, Durkheim argued, by applying his organic, societal "remedy"—his corporatist political-economic model based upon occupational corporations—to the problem of maladjustments.

In his later works, Durkheim came to recognize that his mechanical-organic dichotomy was often too simplistic, and he came to adopt much of Spencer's more complex social evolutionary hierarchy of societal stages. More important, Durkheim recognized that the social fact of heightened functional interdependence among the parts in an increasingly diversified division of labour, even when combined with his corporatist political model, might be insufficient to assure high cohesiveness in the societal whole. Other, more cultural-moral social

TABLE 8.1
Durkheim's Stance on Humans, Existing Societal Organization and the Possibility of Radical Social Change

Human potential	Dualistic—a negative individual side needs to be held in check by a positive social side (–/+)
Existing societal organization	Highly positive, positivist, structuralist, and corporatist (High +)
Possibility of radical social change	Impossible as would only lead to utter anarchy—guided, gradual, positive, evolutionary, corporatist reforms only (High –)

63

facts would have to be found in order to ground societal integration more sufficiently and institutionally in moral authority. Once the societal, structural bases of moral authority were discovered and explained, "moral inculcation," "moral education," or "moral socialization" of the constituent individual and group parts could be systematized.

In *The Elementary Forms of Religious Life* (1912), Durkheim attempted to discover and explain what was most fundamental to the formation of an effective, socially integrating morality in *all* societies. To do this, he examined secondary ethnographic reports of what he argued to be the most "simple" or "primitive" religion in one of the most "simple" or "primitive" societies still in existence, the totemism of the Australian Aborigines. In this way, he attempted to determine the most "elementary" principles underlying what separated the "sacred," or that which was collectively held in awe and forbidden to everyday use, from the "profane," or that which was merely everyday and utilitarian. What he claimed to discover was directly derived from his structuralist-corporatist theory. In social fact, the sacred is such because it is collectively held to be so. The sacred expresses the collective power of the societal body over its lesser parts. Rituals and other institutionalized forms merely recognize and inculcate this societal power over individuals and groups. Again, Durkheim was not at all concerned with individual representations of religiosity, but only with explaining religion structurally, as a collective representation of the *conscience collective*. He did this in order to learn how better to reform society morally so that it could more effectively inculcate a societally integrating morality into its constitutive individuals and groups.

A number of major works published after his death in 1917 demonstrate the less "objective," even more openly social reformist, side of Durkheim's positivist and structuralist corporatism. For instance, in *Moral Education: A Study in the Theory and Application of the Sociology of Education*, Durkheim advanced techniques for the correct socialization of learners in the education system. Through the rigorous and vigorous inculcation of "enthusiasm" for "proper," societally integrating, and not "egoistic" moral values, institutionalized education could inculcate into the young "mental categories" that emphasized a deep respect for the moral authority of society and values that stressed thinking, choosing, and acting for the good of the whole society.

In *Professional Ethics and Civic Morals*, he outlined, in some detail, a program for the gradual introduction into modern society of his fully corporatist polity of rule by across-class occupational corporations. This political corporatism, he argued, followed directly from the "scientific" application of his social theory. In *Socialism and Saint-Simon*, he attempted to distinguish himself from Saint-Simon's utopian or unscientific "socialism" while also discounting Marxism for its emphasis on class struggle and radical transformation.

Durkheim intended and designed his social theory to be a more politically liberal, less state-oriented version of Comte's vision. In opposition to Spencer's economic liberalism and "negative" program of social engineering, Durkheim intended and designed a more "positive" social reformist program that both joined and expanded the sustaining and regulating "functions" of society in a corporatism rooted in moral authority and moral socialization.

Durkheim's consistent denial of the centrality of class contradictions in society paved the way for cross-class "scientific" corporatism and the "moral authority" of society to become central slogans, later in the twentieth century, of liberal and social democratic theories and practices of elite social engineering. In addition, further to the political right, "classless" corporatism and the moral authority of an apparently classless society became the watchwords of some ultraconservative social engineers, such as those in fascist Italy during the 1920s and 1930s. Even on the political left, a version of classless and corporatist moral authority increasingly came to be touted by some of the elite "socialist" or "communist" social engineers who captured state power in the home of the first class-based socialist revolution, the Soviet Union.

Key Sources

Sources for Emile Durkheim's major works include: *The Division of Labour in Society* (Macmillan, 1984); *The Rules of Sociological Method and*

Selected Texts on Sociology and Its Method (Macmillan, 1982); *Suicide: A Study in Sociology* (Free Press, 1964); *The Elementary Forms of Religious Life* (Allen and Unwin, 1976); *Moral Education: A Study in the Theory and Application of the Sociology of Education* (Free Press, 1973); *Professional Ethics and Civic Morals* (Routledge, 1957); and *Socialism* (Collier, 1962).

Steven Lukes, *Emile Durkheim: His Life and Work, a Historical and Critical Study* (Penguin, 1973) and Anthony Giddens, *Emile Durkheim* (Penguin, 1978), give solid overviews of Durkheim's life and theory. Phillip Besnard's *The Sociological Domain: The Durkheimians and the Founding of French Sociology* (Cambridge University Press, 1983) traces Durkheim's huge impact on later social scholarship in France.

Suggestions for Research and Debate

1. Compare (and contrast) Comte's and Durkheim's positivism. To what degree was Durkheim's original?
2. Compare (and contrast) Comte's, Spencer's, and Durkheim's treatments of society as an organism. To what degree was Durkheim original?
3. Contrast Spencer's and Durkheim's views on human nature. How did each view underpin a different form of social reformism?
4. With careful reference to one of Durkheim's works, critically evaluate his conception of morality and normality.
5. Compare (and contrast) Marx's radicalism and Durkheim's reformism. Can corporatism be a part of Marx's Marxism? How so or why not?
6. Theorize why Durkheimian social theory has so often dominated many sociology departments as well as many, apparently different state bureaucracies.

NINE

The Middle Road I: Georg Simmel's Dialectical and Idealist Structuralism and the Forms of Social Interaction

Georg Simmel (1858–1918) was the youngest of seven children born to a wealthy Jewish family in Berlin. His father, a co-owner of a chocolate factory, had converted to Catholicism prior to Georg's birth. He died while Georg was an infant. Fortunately for young Simmel, his guardian, a capitalist who owned a large publishing house, provided him a considerable legacy, which allowed him to live independently for the rest of his life, without need of a steady career.

After graduating from the University of Berlin in philosophy with history and psychology, Simmel was, for almost all his life, unable to secure tenure at a German university because of institutionalized anti-Semitism, petty jealousy over his immense and interdisciplinary productivity and his popularity as a teacher, as well as his own refusal to pander to what he saw as the pretentiousness of the university community. Instead, until near the end of his life, he lectured at the University of Berlin for whatever fees he could attain directly from his student and lay audiences.

Nonetheless, Simmel's financial independence allowed him to enjoy and to connect socially to a full range of cultural achievements in Berlin, which, despite the domination of Prussian militarism and rapid industrialization, was one of the leading centres of avant-garde artistic creativity in Europe. A deep concern for aesthetic creativity within the limitations of a rapidly changing and highly contradictory society is a constant subtext in all his numerous works.

His marginality in, and financial independence from, professional academia probably underpinned another constant subtext in his numerous works, a concern for the centrality to social theorizing of "marginal" topics that often focused on "marginal" people. Certainly, his privileged marginality allowed him to consider both the devastating and the liberating effects of marginality in social relationships.

Georg Simmel was the first person in Germany to publish a book with the word "sociology" in its title and one of the first to teach sociology courses in a German university. Together with Max Weber and a few others, he was responsible for establishing the legitimacy of sociology as a discipline in that country. Like Weber, and all the classical social theorists so far considered, his central concern was with the impact of increasing social differentiation. However, the general value-stance he took in the development of both his "philosophical sociology" and his "pure" or "formal sociology" was shared only by his compatriot Max Weber, whom we will discuss in chapters 10 and 11. As we will argue, Simmel's (and Weber's) value-stance was what we term the middle road with respect to its view of human beings, of existing societal organization, and of the possibility of radical social change—a middle road between the elite engineering stance of both the reformist and neo-liberal varieties, and the Marxist emancipation stance.

In general, Simmel's philosophical sociology attempted to develop a set of *dialectical* and *idealist*, neo-Kantian metatheoretical principles to underpin his more substantive formal sociology. Simmel borrowed this dialectical (processual, interrelated, contradictory) and idealist (idea-categories determine material life) metatheoretical perspective from Hegel's philosophy. He used this perspective to rethink Kant's "categorical imperatives" in human reasoning about, and action within, the external world. Simmel attempted to combine Hegel's dialectical conception of the contradictory unity of the subject/individual and object/external world with Hegel's idealist—mind- or spirit-centred—resolution of that contradictory unity. Simmel did this in order to "socialize," or make social, Kant's epistemology of human reasoning.

In his "critique of pure reason," Kant had argued that human beings could never directly relate to nature or the "external" world; humans could only perceive, reason about, and posit scientifically a coherent order to their *sensations* of that external world. We do this, Kant philosophized, based on a set of internal, a priori or pre-existing "transcendental categories" such as time, space, and causation.

In a chapter entitled "How Is Society Possible?" from a major work that is still not entirely translated, *Sociology: Investigations of Forms of Sociation* (1908), Simmel, like both Hegel and Marx, argues against Kant that the individual's relationships to *social* nature—that is, to other individuals and human creative products—are unlike the individual's relationship to the rest of nature. As individuals, we are not just "outside of" society. We are in dialectical unity with society, both "inside" and "outside"; we both participate within and observe and reason without. In interactions with other individuals, we are both subjects and objects. For Simmel, both "individual and supra-individual [societal] existence" have tendencies towards integration or self-completion; but these ten-

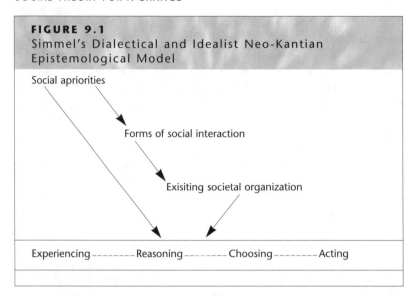

FIGURE 9.1
Simmel's Dialectical and Idealist Neo-Kantian
Epistemological Model

Social apriorities

Forms of social interaction

Exisiting societal organization

Experiencing--------Reasoning--------Choosing--------Acting

dencies can often be opposing and are basically "irreconcilable."

Retaining Kant's own idealism, Simmel accepted that these basic "social" "apriorities" were universal and eternal foundational principles within reasonable humans and that they gradually unfolded in the development of changing "forms of sociation" or human interaction. As such, they shaped, though did not entirely determine, individual self-creation, the creation of social groups, institutions, and societies, and all the content or cultural products within such groups, institutions, and societies.

Like Marx's historical materialism, Simmel's dialectical and idealist neo-Kantianism was developed in order to confront what he saw to be the most fundamental contradiction in human life: the increasing contradiction between individual creativity and the cumulative social product of that creativity—sociocultural organization. However, unlike Marx, Simmel's neo-Kantian apriorities located in each reasoner meant that, to a large degree, "alienation" and the "tragedy of culture" was inevitable. Both the individual and society were constituted in "forms of sociation." Given the apriorities, forms of sociation were necessarily contradictory, both facilitative and constraining of individual self-fulfilment within society.

For Simmel, the increasing gap between the sociocultural objects produced by human creativity and the ability of humans to incorporate these products into new creative expressions was not caused by historical, and thus changeable, social relations. Rather, alienation of the individual in society was caused by the two-sided basis of human

TABLE 9.1
Simmel's Stance on Humans, Existing Societal
Organization and the Possibility of Radical Social
Change

Human potential	Dialectical or two-sided—both creative and alienated—based on two-sided social apriorities (+/–)
Existing societal organization	Dialectical or two-sided—both liberatory and alienating (+/–)
Possibility of radical social change	Impossible—no way to transcend the two-sided nature of both the individual and society (High –)

nature itself, rooted in the universal and unchangeable two-sided social apriorities out of which flowed all social interaction and other socio-cultural production. All contradictions in society were themselves two-sided (+ / –) as a result of the self-contradictory, a priori, idea-categories that were rooted in the two-sided individual (+ / –): being both inside and outside society, being both subject and object, being both self-completing and disintegrated in social development.

In *Sociology: Investigations of Forms of Sociation* and in many other works, Simmel used his social apriorities to ground his pure or formal sociology. Formal sociology was the "science" of the description and, ultimately, explanatory analysis of forms of sociation—that is, of structured patterns of social interaction and association—that mediated between the highly abstract apriorities and concrete living in society. Taken together, these intermediate structural patterns or "forms of sociation" constituted both the individual and society and the existing "web of group affiliations." For Simmel, while the concrete content of human interactions was of immense interest to the historian, biographer, ethnographer, and many other social analysts, the "geometry" of abstract, structural forms of sociation, independent of both the concrete content of the interactions and of individual intentions, was what was important to the sociologist intent on ultimately deriving law-like explanations.

Just as the individual imposed order upon the myriad contents of everyday interactions in order to "make sense" of them, so must the sociologist—only more rigorously. On the basis of a dialectical, two-sided understanding of the social apriorities, the pure sociologist could examine how they work themselves out in "micro-social" forms of sociation and in more "macro-social" networks that constitute the social bases for *necessarily increasing* social differentiation, alienation, and the tragedy of culture.

The most abstract patterning of interaction that Simmel insightfully analysed in order to demonstrate the contradictory, two-sided nature of social interaction, independent of particular content and intentions, was the "quantitative determinateness" or the "geometry" of group structure. Abstract geometric forms that particularly interested Simmel in their shaping of human interaction included number, position, distance, symmetry, and the "intersection of social circles."

With respect to number, Simmel discussed the fundamental changes in the form of interaction necessitated by the apparently simple, numerical addition of one more person to a two-person "dyad." While true interpersonal relations were said to be possible in a dyad, these relations necessarily became much more complex and contradictory in a "triad" or three-person group structure. In a triad, for instance, coalitions of two against one became structurally possible.

Basic geometric changes, such as from a dyad to a triad (and any larger number), shaped numerous other, only slightly less abstract, forms of sociation, such as "superordination and subordination," "conflict," "sociability," and "exchange." More micro-social patterns that Simmel formally analysed included the "secret society," "adornment" or "fashion," "faithfulness and gratitude," and "nobility." The objectification of individuals in forms of sociation included "the stranger," "the coquette," and "the poor."

In all of these forms, Simmel was attuned to examining both how the pattern of social interaction facilitated individual self-fulfilment *and* how the pattern constrained, objectified, or alienated the individual in interaction, based on the two-sided nature of the social apriorities. For example, "the stranger" is an excellent objectification of the apriority that individuals are both inside and outside of society. The stranger is clearly treated as alien; yet this very alien-ness may be the basis for the stranger being entrusted with secrets that would not be shared with non-strangers in the group. On the one hand, the stranger is liberated from social constraints because of his/her outsidedness and can therefore insightfully observe the group. On the other hand, the stranger is objectified into performing only a delimited participatory role in the group or society.

Simmel's most complete and extensive discussion of the two-sidedness of social interactional forms was his *The Philosophy of Money* (1900). In this major work, Simmel draws upon Marx's analysis, in volume 1 of *Capital* and elsewhere, of money as the exemplar of the reduction of all human values to mere exchange value. Following Marx, Simmel argues that money, having no value other than its exchangeability for any other value, increasingly comes to determine the actual value of all human creativity by its ability to set the cash-value (the price) of all relationships and cultural products.

However, as opposed to Marx, who argued that this increasing objectification of humanity was rooted in the concrete, historically developing class struggle over the value of labour power, Simmel argued that money was merely the abstract expression of the objectification that necessarily accompanied greater social differentiation in an expanding human population. Indeed, Simmel argued, in direct opposition to Marx, that money was a social form that could also, to a degree, liberate individuals by, for instance, allowing them an increased variety of purchasing choices within an increasingly integrated world of commerce and exchange or by allowing them the chance to interact, if only through what Marx called the "cash nexus," with many more individuals from other cultures.

> The importance of the money economy for individual liberty is enhanced if we explore the form that the persistent relations of dependence actually possess. As already indicated, the money economy makes possible not only a solution but a specific kind of mutual dependence which, at the same time, affords room for a maximum of liberty. Firstly, on the face of it, it creates a series of previously unknown obligations. Dependency upon third persons has spread into completely new areas ever since a considerable amount of working capital, mostly in terms of mortgages, had to be sunk into the soil in order to wrest from it the required yield. Such dependency upon third parties also spreads once tools that were directly produced with raw materials are produced indirectly by certain amounts of prefabricated components and once the labourer uses the means of production which he does not own. The more the activity and life of people becomes dependent upon objective conditions by virtue of a complicated technology, the greater necessarily is the dependence upon more and more people. However, these people gain their significance for the individual concerned solely as representatives of those functions, such as owners of capital and suppliers of working materials. What kind of people they are in other respects plays no role here.

In *The Philosophy of Money*, *both* the facilitative and the constraining aspects of money-exchange were viewed within an overriding context of a deepening tragedy of culture. Human creativity, or "subjective culture," was necessarily being overwhelmed and dominated by the rapidly increasing mass of "objective culture." Ultimately, Simmel saw no way out of the increased objectification or alienation of humanity.

Simmel's ahistorical idealism disallowed the possibility of history-making, collective, and self-emancipatory action by the most alienated. For Marx, the contradiction between human creativity and alienating society was actually transformable, in favour of human creativity, through the self-emancipatory class struggles of, especially, the most exploited and oppressed. For Simmel, all collectivities were necessarily two-sided and therefore never liberatory as such. Indeed, as he explicitly argues in *The Philosophy of Money*, Marxist-inspired socialist collective actions actually quicken the inevitable process of the tragedy of culture at a greater rate than does money-exchange. For Simmel, such actions must always bury the subjective culture of each in favour of the objective culture of all.

In Simmel's theory, transformative self-emancipatory action simply was not possible by the individual, given his belief in the eternal/ahistorical and universal/necessary, two-sided nature of human beings, forms of sociation, and society. More importantly this theoretical approach disallowed any collective social vehicle of self-emancipation from travelling along the emancipatory lane of the two-sided middle road. Over the long haul, Simmel's middle road theory ends up in a dead end.

Key Sources

Selections from Georg Simmel's *Sociology: Investigations of Forms of Sociation* are included in his *Conflict and the Web of Group Affiliations* (Free Press, 1964), in Kurt H. Wolff's editions of *The Sociology of Georg Simmel* (Free Press, 1950) and *Essays on Sociology, Philosophy, and Aesthetics by Georg Simmel et al.* (Harper and Row, 1959), and in Donald E. Levine's edition of *Georg Simmel: On Individuality and Social Forms* (University of Chicago Press, 1971). Simmel's *The Philosophy of Money* (Routledge and Kegan Paul, 1978) should be a must read in sociology because of both its strengths and weaknesses.

David Frisby's *Georg Simmel* (Tavistock, 1984) and his *Simmel and Since: Essays on Simmel's Social Theory* (Routledge and Kegan Paul, 1992) provide good overviews of Simmel's theory, its historical context, and its later impact.

Suggestions for Research and Debate

1. Compare (and contrast) Simmel's conception of social apriorities to Durkheim's conception of social facts. Which is more incisive? Why?

2. Compare (and contrast) Simmel's concept of alienation to that of Marx. Which is more incisive? Why?

3. Discuss one particular micro-social form of interaction, such as fashion. Why is a two-sided approach that shows the "good" and the "bad" so attractive initially? What are its drawbacks?

4. Discuss Simmel's two-sided "middle road" as the theoretical expression of his own circumstances of lifelong privileged marginality. Which affected his social theory more? His being privileged? His being marginal?

5. Can a social theory rooted in universal and eternal principles ever be emancipatory? How or why not?

TEN

Born in Erfurt, Saxony, Max Weber (1864–1920), like Georg Simmel, grew up in inherited wealth. His paternal grandfather had co-founded a successful linen firm; his maternal grandfather had been a high-ranking Prussian civil servant. Max's earthy, authoritarian father was a long-sitting legislator in both the Prussian House of Deputies and, later, in the Imperial Parliament (Reichstag) of a unified Germany for the centre-right National Liberal Party. His mother was a devout and ethically strict Protestant. The attempt to find a middle road reconciling the compromising earthiness and authoritarianism of his bureaucratic father, on the one side, and the otherworldly, ascetic religiosity of his mother, on the other, marked Max Weber's entire life and scholarship and has been much remarked upon in commentaries.

Weber initially followed his father's footsteps into jurisprudence and dissolute living. However, by the time he had received his doctorate in jurisprudence, with an emphasis on political economy, from the University of Berlin and had become a professor of economics at the University of Freiburg, Weber had become infamous for his disciplined and ascetic, though not overtly Christian, lifestyle. In 1897, in the middle of his life, Max Weber suffered a complete emotional collapse after the loss of his father, who had died shortly after Weber had confronted him for being a tyrant and abusing his mother. With the nurturance of his spouse, Marianne, he was able to recover enough to resume a highly productive scholarly career as the Chair of Political Science at the University of Heidelberg.

Less remarked upon in most commentaries is the fact that, throughout his adult life, Weber was a nationalist who supported a Greater Germany. He was a lifelong contributing member of the Association for Social Policy, a German nationalist political economy think tank. In his inaugural lecture at the University of Freiburg in 1895, he argued that

German economic policy must be judged by only "*German* standards": "The *power* interests of the nation are, wherever they are in question, the ultimate decisive interests that must be served by the nation's economic policy."

As well, Weber was an officer in the Reserve Corps of the German army. During the First World War, he argued in favour of Imperial German expansion "for *honour*" and as a counterweight in middle Europe to Russian bureaucratic and authoritarian tsarism to the east and Anglo-Saxon economic imperialism to the west. He railed against the anti-war, Marxist internationalist wing of the German Social Democratic Party, which was co-led by Rosa Luxemburg (whom we will discuss in chapter 14), and called for its rapid suppression. After the war, he helped draft a new, somewhat democratic constitution for the Weimar Republic, although by then he had lost any hope in creating and maintaining a Greater Germany without a strong leader.

In 1903, Weber had co-founded a scholarly journal dedicated to "the historical and theoretical recognition of the general cultural significance of capitalist development," the central problem of all his subsequent scholarly work. With Georg Simmel, among others, Weber co-founded the German Sociological Society in 1910, thus helping to institutionalize sociology as a separate discipline in Germany.

Like Marx and Simmel, Weber accepted a dialectical/relational view of humans in society in which both the individual and the society were constituted in social relations. Like Marx, Weber stressed the creative, intentional potential of human beings. Also like Marx, he stressed a *historical* understanding and explanation, rooted in particular times and spaces, a social world of creative, intentional humanity.

But Weber also fully accepted Immanuel Kant's strict separation between the natural and the social-moral world, and he therefore accepted that knowledge of these "two" worlds had to be fundamentally different. The neo-Kantian Georg Simmel, we can recall, had attempted a strictly *philosophical*, idealist, a priori bridging of these forms of knowledge, which would, he argued, ultimately allow universal and eternal, law-like statements about the social-moral world. Weber, on the other hand, accepted the Kantian philosophic divide between natural and social-moral knowledge and sought a historically rooted solution to the problem of valid and reliable knowledge in the social sciences.

Because, for Weber (as for Marx), knowledge of the social-moral world of human beings must be rooted in particular times and sociocultural spaces, "nomothetic"—universal—and eternal laws derived from "objective," positivist, natural scientific practices were either inappropriate to the explanation of the social world or, at best, were trivial. But, as a Kantian, Weber also rejected both Hegel's idealist, dialectical unification of nature within Spirit *and* Marx's materialist, dialectical unification of the two worlds through contradictory, creative human practice.

Weber's development of his *historical-idealist* theoretical approach has justifiably earned him membership in the Big Three of classical sociological theory, along with Marx and Durkheim. His social theory was explicitly developed as a social-scientific middle road between rational determinism and irrational voluntarism. On the rational-determinist side, Weber reacted against the social determinism of Spencer and Durkheim. Also, he explicitly rejected economic determinism, which, restricting himself to secondary sources and the dominant practice of the German Social Democratic Party, he mistook to be the essential feature of Marx's historical materialism.

On the voluntarist side, Weber rejected *perspectivism*, the view that all assertions about truth and meaning are simply relative claims reflecting one's own perspective. In its extreme, anti-democratic form, as argued by Friedrich Nietzsche, perspectivism was rooted in irrational "drives": "Every drive is a kind of lust to rule; each one has its perspective that it would like to compel all the other drives to accept as a norm." In Nietzsche's nihilistic, or extremely sceptical, perspective, what was generally held to be true and meaningful was merely the result of the imposition of the irrational "will to power" upon rational-looking interpretations of truth and meaning.

For Weber, "The world in which we ourselves exist intellectually is largely a world stamped by Marx [on the one side] and Nietzsche [on the other side]." Weber modified the nineteenth-century German *historicist* intellectual tradition in order to pave a historical-idealist theoretical path between Marx and Nietzsche. German historicism had itself developed as a cultural-nationalist response to political-economic proponents of universal "rational man," on the one hand, and to the reduction of human history to the drives of great persons, on the other.

The historicist Wilhelm Dilthey, for instance, had argued that intentional human creativity must always be understood in terms of its specific, intended meaning. Since another's exact personal experiences were never knowable as such, *verstehen*—understanding of intended meaning—had to rely on "interpretation." The interpretive approach of *hermeneutics* was being developed in literary studies in order to understand the author's intended meaning through the analysis of the textual product. Hermeneutics could, Dilthey argued, be generalized to the interpretive understanding of the individual's intended meaning by a situated analysis of his or her surrounding "cultural objects," including social groups, institutions, and the national culture.

But, whereas historicists such as Dilthey had emphasized the interpretive method primarily as a means of understanding individual intentions, Weber argued that social analysis must be meaningful not only in the sense of capturing the intended meaning of the individual actors. Social analysis must also be meaningful in the sense of producing *general* categories of meaningful action that were generalizable within the specific time and cultural space in which they were developed and that were *comparable* to other general categories produced in other times or cultures.

Weber, therefore, set out to define theoretically the middle road between determinism and voluntarism, between positivism and historicism. In a series of essays contained in *The Methodology of the Social Sciences* (1903–17), he attempted to do this by theoretically grounding and adapting Dilthey's concept of *ideal types* to forms of social action that could serve as the basis for the interpretive analysis of larger, societal-level institutions and other cultural contents. Weber's ideal types were meant to be situated, but nevertheless generalizable and comparable, categories or "idea-types" of meaningful social action. Such ideal types could be utilized, Weber argued, both as heuristic devices, or "eureka-helpers," for reliable and valid interpretation and also for non-positivistic causal analysis, insofar as causality connoted only the high likelihood that one social event will be accompanied or followed by another.

Although this point has often been missed in the commentaries, for Weber ideal types were not to be derived from the expressed, conscious intentions of the social actors being investigated. Instead, ideal types were to be drawn from the cultural system of shared meanings that surrounded and conditioned the intentions of social actors, in particular from the surrounding national and religious cultures. The *individual* intentions that Weber argued had to be recognized and admitted in the development of ideal types were those of the analyst, not those of the individual actor per se. Thus, "An ideal type is formed by the one-sided *accentuation* of one or more points of view and by the synthesis of a great many diffuse, discrete, more or less present and occasionally absent *concrete individual* phenomena, which are arranged according to those one-sidedly emphasized viewpoints into a unified *analytical* construct." Based on the analyst's intentions or perspective, ideal types were intended to highlight features of meaningful social action that were held to be important. They were explicitly not supposed to represent the real or, a fortiori, material "essence" of the actions under consideration. They were ideal only in the strict sense of being an idea, a "mental construct" that "in its conceptual purity" "cannot be found empirically anywhere in reality." Their scientific utility depended on their heuristic value and upon their causal, in the sense of statistically probable, explanatory power.

In the development of his ideal *types of social action*, finally published posthumously in *Economy and Society* (1921), Max Weber, in his relentless search for the middle road, chose to highlight both the rational and the irrational bases for meaningful social action. Weber advanced a four-part, ideal typology of meaningful social action. Two of the types were seen as rational; two were seen as non-rational.

The first type of rational social action was *Zweckrational* or *rationally purposeful* instrumental action. Rationally purposeful action was said to occur when individuals attempted to utilize the most effective means, or instruments, for the attainment of preconceived goals. This type of action is "determined by expectations as to the behaviour of objects in the environment and of other human beings; these expectations are used as 'conditions' or 'means' for the attainment of the actor's own rationally pursued and calculated ends." A good example of this type would be the so-called economic man of mainstream economics who steadfastly pursues the most efficient path to his own satisfaction or enrichment; another example would be the "objective" scientists who efficiently developed the atomic bomb without, in the main, ever questioning the goal.

The second type of rational action, *Vertrational* or *value-rational* action, stressed the attainment of reasoned goals over the mere instrumental efficiency of means to preconceived ends. According to Weber, such action is "determined by a conscious belief in the value for its own sake of some ethical, aesthetic, religious, or other form of behaviour, independently of its prospects for success." It was most probably Max Weber's—and his mother's—preferred type of human action (and, to the extent that choices are directly addressed and made problematic, it is included in our ERCA epistemological model). With the ideal type of value-rational action, Weber attacked, theoretically, the economistic and scientistic reduction of all rational human action to only one type—the instrumentalist, *Zweckrational* glorification of efficiency.

Weber theorized his two other ideal types of social action as non-rational: *affective* and *traditional* action. Affective action is said to be determined by the emotional state of the actor. Expressing these emotions becomes an end in itself and the means to that expression are not rationally considered. Traditional action, for Weber, is directly determined by habitual custom. Both the ends and the means are culturally fixed and are taken for granted by the actor. Why cultural determination and taken-for-grantedness should make traditional action non-rational is, of course, highly problematic. Surely, for instance, the high degree of cultural determination in pre-market, pre-capitalist social formations does not mean that they are non-rational; such formations were clearly rational from the point of view of at least the winners in the system, providing a means of securing valued ends.

At any rate, Weber clearly recognized that any concrete social action

FIGURE 10.1
Weber's Ideal Typical Epistemological Model

Existing societal organization

Experiencing --------- Reasoning -------- Choosing -------- Acting

4 Types of social action

Zweckrational or rationally purposeful action stressing rational choices of means to pre-established ends.
Vertrational or value-rational action stressing rational choices of ends.
Affective action stressing an irrational/unreasoned leap from experience to action based on emotions.
Traditional action stressing an irrational/unreasoned choice of action based on culturally determined means and ends.

would, in reality, contain a combination of all four ideal types. Thus all social action would, in actuality, be both rational and irrational. As indicated in the Figure 10.1, the first two types of action represent a full ERCA process, differing mainly in the stress on means or on ends. The other two types omit parts of the ERCA process. Affective action leaves out both reasoning and choosing, while Weber posited that traditional action leaves out reasoning.

Weber was particularly concerned with the probable effectiveness of social action. In *Economy and Society*, he defined *power* as "the probability that one actor within a social relationship will be in a position to carry out his own will despite resistance." *Domination* was defined in a similar way, being the "probability that certain specific commands (or all commands) will be obeyed by a given group of persons." For Weber, "'classes,' 'status groups,' and 'parties' are phenomena of the distribution of power within a community."

Weber agreed with Marx that class was a determinant of one's powerfulness or powerlessness in social action. However, in contrast to Marx, Weber treated class as a merely economic "position" in society and as an idea-type, not a material relationship with real collective consequences. As well, in contrast to Marx, Weber treated class as only one of three, not necessarily related, bases for power, though he admitted that in the real world one's class position was often the determinant base.

Weber's second basis for powerfulness or powerlessness in social action was, he argued, rooted in actual social communities, unlike class. One's *status situation* was defined as "every typical component of the life of men that is determined by a specific, positive or negative, social estimation of *honour.*" Differing "status groups" were seen as exhibiting different lifestyles, sometimes independently of class position.

The third basis for powerfulness or powerlessness in social action, unlike one's economically defined class position and one's socially defined status position, was seen as necessarily socially organized. *Parties* were defined as "always *structures* struggling for domination." Parties, therefore, were seen as always political or power-oriented, whether existing in state institutions or in local clubs. Indeed, parties were always organized political groups seeking domination or obedience to their agenda within social settings.

With these notions of power and domination, Weber proceeded to develop an ideal typification of authority. For Weber, *authority* was simply "legitimate," as opposed to illegitimate, domination. Since for Weber, legitimate domination was simply domination that was socially *legitimated,* or regularly obeyed, he, in effect, conflated authority and domination.

The *state* secured its dominant position of authority over society by establishing its "*monopoly* of the *legitimate* use of physical force in the enforcement of its order." Thus, like Marx, Weber saw the state as rooted in coercion. However, Marx had argued against the legitimacy of every state that was ruled by a minority class and, indeed, had theorized that the very existence of any coercive state under real conditions of classless communism was illegitimate. Against Marx (and like Nietzsche and, as we will see, Vilfredo Pareto), Weber argued that the legitimacy of the coercive state depended not on its class basis but simply upon its ability to dominate effectively, without massive opposition.

Lastly, in *Economy and Society* Weber related his four ideal types of social action to his ideal typification of authority in order to theorize three ideal typical ways in which authority structures were legitimated. The traditional type of social action was seen as grounding, ideal typically, *traditional authority* based on "an established belief in the sanctity of immemorial traditions and the legitimacy of those exercising authority under them." *Zweckrational* or instrumental, rational-purposeful action grounded *rational-legal authority* based on "a belief in the legality of enacted rules and the right of those elevated to authority under such rules to issue commands." Its prototypical expression was seen to be *bureaucracy,* based on the implementation of a clearly defined set of rules for a hierarchy of clearly defined offices from which the occupants draw their authority.

The third type of authority structure, *charismatic authority*, is particularly interesting because it is grounded in two ideal types of social action: the irrational, affective type and the *Vertrational* or value-rational type. For Weber, charismatic authority rested on two bases. First, effective "charisma" (which in classical Greek meant "grace") or emotive leadership qualities of the charismatic individual rested upon emotional affects. Second, the values to which the charismatic leader appealed were said to be rooted in rationally held values.

Why, you might ask, did Weber, following his own arguments for ideal types, not ground charismatic authority in affective social action only? Since ideal types were not supposed to be real but were intended only to highlight, why was charismatic authority not made consistent with the other two types and grounded in only one type of action? And why did he not put forward a fourth ideal type of authority structure rooted solely (or, in real terms, primarily) in value-rational social action? Weber failed to do so, despite the resulting inconsistency with his own theory, because, I propose, his deep anti-Marxism caused him to deny even the possibility that legitimate, authoritative action could ever be taken *collectively* by the vast majority of people based on reasoned and collectively shared self-emancipatory values (such as pro-socialist and anti-capitalist values). As we will see in the next chapter, Weber's failure even to allow, theoretically, for the possibility of reasoned, collective self-emancipation was to befuddle and, in the end, undermine both his theorization of historical process and his own value-stance on the fundamental creativity of human beings.

Key Sources

The main sources referred to in this chapter are Max Weber's essays contained in *The Methodology of the Social Sciences* (Free Press, 1949) and his three-volume *Economy and Society* (Bedminster Press, 1968).

Marianne Weber's *Max Weber: A Biography* (Wiley, 1975) provides important details of Weber's life as interpreted by his spouse. In *Politics and Sociology in the Thought of Max Weber* (Macmillan, 1972), Anthony Giddens places Weber's theory in the political context of his period, while Wolfgang J. Mommsen and Jurgen Osterhammel's edition of *Max Weber and His Contemporaries* (Allen and Unwin, 1987) relates Weber to other intellectuals of his time.

Those wishing to examine some primary-source material on German historicism might try Wilhelm Dilthey, *Selected Writings* (Cambridge University Press, 1976). Those wishing more on anti-democratic perspectivism should try Friedrich Nietzsche's *The Will to Power* (Random House, 1967).

Suggestions for Research and Debate

1. Discuss a local, contemporary social action setting, such as your social theory classroom, in terms of the four ideal types of social action. Can this setting be captured adequately in terms of a single

type of rationality or irrationality? Why or why not?

2. Discuss yourself in terms of the four ideal types of social action. Can your actions be captured adequately in terms of a single type of rationality or irrationality? Why or why not?

3. Critically evaluate a local, contemporary authority, such as your university's president, in terms of the type of authority structure underlying his or her legitimated domination.

4. Theorize what a structure of authority that is underpinned by value-rational social action might look like. What would be its relationship to other types of authority structure?

5. Which type of social action would you want to typify your actions? Why? Which type of authority structure would you like to be dominated by? Why?

The Middle Road IIb: Weber's Theory of Rationalization and the Prospects for Social Change

ELEVEN

Max Weber's extensive historical and comparative research into the initial rise of capitalism in western Europe and its increasingly global domination represents the clearest and best attempt to develop a middle road theory in classical sociology—a theory that could adequately trace a path between glorifying the existing state of social organization, on the one side, and advocating its radical transformation, on the other. As such, his arguments merit close attention, since they have influenced virtually every later attempt to find a middle road between elite engineering and emancipatory, self-conscious, revolutionary social transformation.

As we have seen in the previous chapter, Weber had consciously positioned his own theory of social change between the theories of the two men he considered to be the greatest social thinkers of the nineteenth century, his fellow Germans Karl Marx and Friedrich Nietzsche. Against Nietzsche's individualist and authoritarian perspectivism, Weber substituted a focus on shared meaningfulness. Against Marx's materialist realism, Weber substituted his ideal(ist) typification.

Weber also attacked the positivism of elite engineering theories because of its uncritical reduction of all types of meaningfulness to merely *Zweckrational* principles. For Weber, positivism's blindness to its own scientistic-technological bias underpinned its uncritical attitude to social organization based upon these rationally purposeful principles.

Weber was especially opposed to what he saw, often correctly, to be the positivist economism of his "Marxist" contemporaries. Weber's stress on the active contribution of societal-level culture to social change was intended to correct this perceived economism in Marxism. In *The Protestant Ethic and the Spirit of Capitalism* (1904–05), for instance, Weber attacked the economistic Marxist argument that ideas were merely a product of the existing mode of production. Instead,

Weber overtly argued, *as had Marx before him*, that "ideational" (or, for Marx, ideological/superstructural) and "material" factors were interrelated and interdependent in the historical development of capitalism. Thus, Weber agreed with Marx's historical materialism with respect to the interrelationship and interdependence of ideological and material factors.

Yet Weber disagreed with and attempted to supersede Marx's historical materialism by overtly giving ideational factors a theoretically equal causal status with material factors in the rise of capitalism. While recognizing the interrelationship and interdependence of both sets of factors, Marx had given theoretical priority to material forces over ideological forces in the final analysis. As well, Weber's ideal typifications of Protestantism and capitalism, for example, were antithetical to Marx's materialist theory *and* to Weber's own claims for the interrelationship and interdependence of ideational and material factors, insofar as such concepts were thoroughly idealist, being derived from ethical/spiritual meaning systems that were regularly treated as unrelated to class forces.

Having first established the statistical over-representation of Protestants in capitalist endeavours in western Europe and the United States, *The Protestant Ethic and the Spirit of Capitalism* addressed itself not to the class nature of both capitalism and Protestantism but to ethical/spiritual meaning-orientation behind both. In this work, Weber's central argument is the high degree to which the *Protestant ethic*, as an ideal type, historically facilitated, however unintentionally, the rapid and ongoing development of an ideal typical *spirit of capitalism*. Ironically, Weber argued, the spirit of capitalism, once established, was increasingly smothering the very Protestant ethic that had facilitated its emergence.

For Weber, Protestantism's doctrine of the unmediated "priesthood of all believers" had left adherents to face an unknowable God alone, without the external institutional or ritualistic support available to Catholics. This individualized uncertainty concerning one's relationship to God facilitated in Protestants, according to Weber, a rational and methodical inner monitoring and supervision of one's lifestyle as a means of attaining some sense of God's grace upon oneself. For particular Protestant sects—such as Calvinists, who believed in God's unknowable predestination of the saved and the damned—the uncertainty of one's relation to God was even more intense and anxiety producing and thus required an even more methodical inner accounting of one's lifestyle.

For Weber, the intense uncertainty of each Protestant's relationship to the Supreme Being led to the development of the Protestant ethic, an ideal typical *ascetic* orientation to everyday life in this world that encouraged disciplined hard work, thrift, and righteous godliness as indirect indications of God's saving grace. This ethic of methodical self-denial came to provide, according to Weber, the principal ideational underpinning, despite its purported otherworldly focus, for the profoundly this-worldly, ideal typical spirit of capitalism, which stressed self-interested, methodical planning and reinvestment in order to maximize profits and ensure ongoing capital accumulation. Thus, not otherworldly asceticism as such but worldly economic success provided the remedy for individual salvation anxiety.

Weber's later studies of Confucianism and Taoism in *The Religion of China: Confucianism and Taoism* (1916) and of Hinduism and Buddhism in *The Religion of India: The Sociology of Hinduism and Buddhism* (1916–17) underscored the uniqueness of the western European Protestant ethic as the central ideational condition that facilitated the initial development of capitalism in western Europe and the United States. Despite, in many instances, better material conditions for the development of rational capitalism in other major civilizations, Weber argued that the religious conditions in these other societies militated against the emergence of the spirit of capitalism. In *Ancient Judaism* (1917–19) Weber emphasized the specifically ethical-rationalist basis of Judaism's notion of a single God and a Chosen People as an early ideational progenitor of the Protestant ethic and, thence, the spirit of capitalism.

In *The Protestant Ethic and the Spirit of Capitalism*, Weber had documented a process in which an unworldly, value-rational Protestant ethic had led to a strictly worldly rational-purposeful spirit of constant capital accumulation. Tragically for Weber, this rationally purposeful spirit of capitalism was rapidly smothering the value-rational Protestant ethic and all other forms of meaningful action.

> The Puritan wanted to work in a calling; we are forced to do so. For when asceticism was carried out of monastic cells into everyday life, and began to dominate worldly morality, it did its part in building the tremendous cosmos of the modern economic order. This order is now bound to the technical and economic conditions of machine production which today determine the lives of all the individuals who are born into this mechanism, not only those directly concerned with economic acquisition, with irresistible force. Perhaps it will so determine them until the last ton of fossilized coal is burnt. In [the English Puritan] Baxter's view the care for external goods should only lie on the shoulders of the "saint like a light cloak, which can be thrown aside at any moment." But fate decreed that the cloak should become an iron cage.
>
> Since asceticism undertook to remodel the world and to work out its ideas in the world, material goods have gained an increasing and finally

an inexorable power over the lives of men as at no previous period in history. Today the spirit of religious asceticism—whether finally, who knows?—has escaped from the cage. But victorious capitalism, since it rests on mechanical foundations, needs its support no longer. The rosy blush of its laughing heir, the Enlightenment, seems also to be irretrievably fading, and the idea of duty in one's calling prowls about in our lives like the ghost of dead religious beliefs. Where the fulfilment of the calling cannot directly be related to the highest spiritual and cultural values, or when, on the other hand, it need not be felt simply as economic compulsion, the individual generally abandons the attempt to justify it at all. In the field of its highest development, in the United States, the pursuit of wealth, stripped of its religious and ethical meaning, tends to become associated with purely mundane passions, which often actually give it the character of sport.

No one knows who will live in this cage in the future, or whether at the end of this tremendous development entirely new prophets will arise, or there will be a great rebirth of old ideas and ideals, or, if neither, mechanized petrification, embellished with a sort of convulsive self-importance. For of the last stage of this cultural development, it might be truly said: "Specialists without spirit, sensualists without heart; this nullity imagines that it has attained a level of civilization never before achieved."

The historical rise to domination of the spirit of capitalism over the Protestant ethic represented, for Weber, just one instance, no matter how important, of the more general historical rise to domination of the *Zweckrational* or rationally purposeful ideal type over the *Vertrational* or value-rational ideal type of authoritative social action. *Zweckrational* action was becoming increasingly dominant throughout the entire world as the only authoritative type of social action. For Weber this process was ultimately unstoppable—it was "escape-proof."

This historical process of the increasing domination of the *Zweckrational*, based on its high cost-benefit efficiencies through the rapid adjustment of means to serve preconceived ends, Weber termed *rationalization*. Rationalization or, to be more precise, "*Zweckrational*-ization" was seen to increasingly dominate all aspects of meaningful human life. It was apparent in the domination of positivist science and technologism in authoritative thinking; in bureaucratization of the state and in the state's application of social engineering techniques to increase the efficiency of social administration for capital accumulation and citizen control; in the formal systematization and unification of culture, including art and music; and in the increased rational-legal routinization of everyday life.

For Weber, this inevitable, escape-proof "steel-hard cage" of single-type rationalization was transforming human creative potential into the "nullity" of the faceless but efficient bureaucrat or corporate manager. Active, creative human potential (+) was becoming a single-minded, and therefore creatively mindless, mass (–) due to the increasing domination of only one type of meaningful activity, *Zweckrational* instrumentalism. As social organization became increasingly instrumental, social life increasingly became like a kind of steel-hard cage that had the tragic capacity to shrink. Thus, *Zweckrational* instrumentalism was gradually and, for Weber, inevitably smothering any degree of freedom in human reasoning, choice, and social action.

Faced with the profound pessimism of his own theory of the historical development of a *Zweckrational*-ization that had now become inevitable, what, for Weber, were the prospects for personal escape from the abhorrent steel-hard cage? According to Weber, all that was available to individuals, who were increasingly condemned by rationalization to lose all sense of autonomy and self-worth, was a survival flight back to either of the two major modes of transcendental, religious experience that Weber had documented in his works on religions. Individuals could still survive in the cage by choosing "mysticism," a flight away from the everyday world through a change in one's state of consciousness, no matter how induced. Alternatively, individuals could still survive in the cage by choosing "asceticism," selflessly applying themselves to mastering some task performance without concern for rewards or pleasures. In either case, the enveloping cage of societal rationalization would not disappear; all that would change is the individual's attitude to life in the cage. As evidenced in his life work as well as in his article "Science as a Vocation," Weber's personal choice was an ascetic commitment to social science.

With respect to the prospects of radical societal transformation, Weber was forced, by the logic of his own historical-idealist theoretical approach to the development of capitalism, to be even more pessimistic. For Weber, socialism could never be a transformative alternative to rationalization because socialism was necessarily economistic and thus was an even higher form of rationalized social engineering than capitalism, an even more smothering and necessarily bureaucratic steel-hard cage of rationalization. While this criticism of socialism was true, in the main, of socialism in his time (as well as of much of later Soviet Union–style socialism), it conveniently ignored Marx's historical-materialist theorization of the self-emancipation of the working class.

Indeed, with respect to Marx's actual Marxism, as opposed to the economism of many later "Marxists," Weber's middle road theory did much more than merely supplement an economistic Marxism with an idealist emphasis on cultural forces. Weber denied, conceptually and theoretically, the possibility of materially rooted *Vertrational* social action. In denying collectively shared *and* individually self-conscious

TABLE 11.1
Weber's Stance on Humans, Existing Societal Organization, and the Possibility of Radical Social Change

Human potential	The full range of meaningful social actions has become reduced to only one type of meaningfulness (+ becomes –)
Existing societal organization	Increasingly is a steel-hard cage of rationalization (–)
Possibility of radical social change	Impossible given the increasing domination of rationalization (high –)

value-rational action based on real conditions of inequality as a meaningful basis for authoritative social action, Weber gutted the real possibility of massive self-emancipation.

By denying the centrality, and indeed the very reality, of class, class consciousness, and class struggle to social action, Weber threw away the best-theorized key to unlock the door leading to the collective self-emancipation of humanity from exploitation and systemic oppression. He threw away this key despite what we have already seen to be his initially highly favourable view of human potential (+), and despite his severe critique of contemporary societal organization (–). In place of Marx's class self-emancipatory key, Weber substituted ideal types of cultural meaningfulness that were unequally distributed among the "great" national-religious cultures of the world. Weber thereby not only gutted the class-rooted materialism and the emancipatory potential of Marx's Marxism, but also its internationalism.

Having denied even the possibility of authoritative, collective and internationalist *Vertrational* social action against the rising global tide of *Zweckrational* instrumentalism, Weber was forced to place his hopes for a societal alternative to rationalization on affective irrationalism. Especially after the defeat of Germany in the First World War, Weber advocated the return to imperial power of a Greater Germany based on the leadership of a charismatic leader. In this way, Weber provided a set of liberal democratic arguments that could and would be used to justify the rise to power, after Weber's death, of that ideal typical anti-Enlightenment figure, Adolf Hitler.

Weber, however, did realize that irrationally rooted, charismatic leadership could, at best, provide only temporary relief from the inevitable onslaught of rationalization. Charismatic authority was highly likely to become routinized into traditional authority or, more usually, into rational-legal, *Zweckrational* authority. In other words, for Weber, there were no real prospects for societal change (–), apart from the ongoing and now inevitable historical process towards a dehumanized, fully rationalized end-game.

Thus, having wanted to theorize a middle road between Nietzschean irrational perspectivism on the one side and positivist social engineering and socialist transformation on the other, Weber's middle road concluded at a dead end. Having ignored the core of Marx's Marxism, Weber had dallied with the anti-rational, anti-Enlightenment possibility of national salvation through a Nietzschean "superman," but he knew this to be, at best, only a temporary solution.

Having begun with a value-stance that stressed human potential and the non-radical reform of oppressive societal conditions (+ – –), Weber had argued himself into a value stance that was totally hopeless and/or suicidal from both individual and societal perspectives (– – –). With *Zweckrational*-ization, human potential had become almost entirely stifled by rationalization. "The disenchantment of the world" was now all but complete. Not only did *Zweckrational*-ization disenchant the world from all magic, it also robbed the world of human potential, turning humanity into pre-programmed, robotic instruments of a single, unstoppable, instrumentalist meaning system.

The strength of Weber's attempt to map out a theoretical middle road that would not be socialist and not be irrationalist ultimately ended in an ascetic, self-disciplined survivalist attitude to the cage of rationalization. Despite being the most extensive and intensive effort in classical sociology to theorize a middle road between apologetic social engineering and social revolution, Weber's own conclusions were to demonstrate that there was no middle road. It is up to the reader to determine whether Weber's impasse is merely ironic, or whether it is symptomatic of social reality.

Key Sources

Besides the previously cited *Economy and Society*, works by Max Weber consulted for this chapter include: *The Protestant Ethic and the Spirit of Capitalism* (Scribner's, 1958); *The Religion of China: Confucianism and Taoism* (Macmillan, 1964); *The Religion of India: The Sociology of Hinduism and Buddhism* (Free Press, 1958); *Ancient Judaism* (Free Press, 1952); and H.H. Gerth and C. Wright Mills's edition of *From Max Weber: Essays in Sociology* (Oxford University Press, 1974).

For debates on Weber's relationship to other social theorists, see Otto Stammer's edition of *Max Weber and Sociology Today* (Harper Torchbooks,

1972) and Robert J. Antonio and Ronald M. Glassman's *A Weber–Marx Dialogue* (University of Kansas Press, 1985).

Suggestions for Research and Debate

1. Discuss aspects of the historical interplay between religion and capitalism from a Weberian historical idealist stance, from a Durkheimian positivist and structuralist stance, and from a Marxist historical materialist stance. Which approach is most adequate? Why?

2. Discuss how rationalization is pervasive in all contemporary social life. Does its pervasiveness mean that rationalization is the end of human history? Or is there a possible way out of the "steel-hard cage"? If not, what is to be done? If so, how?

3. Try to convince Max Weber not to commit suicide on the basis of his conclusions, by convincing him that his theory and analyses do provide for a viable middle road.

4. Try to convince Max Weber that he ought to be content with individualist solutions, such as asceticism or mysticism, to the life within the steel-hard cage. Show why your arguments would be unacceptable to him.

5. Try to convince Max Weber that his own arguments should have led him to become a Marxist social theorist in order to facilitate human potential through radical social change. Show why your arguments would be unacceptable to him.

Elite Engineering IV: Vilfredo Pareto's Anti-Enlightenment Irrationalism, Sentiments, and the Circulation of Elites

TWELVE

Born in Paris, Vilfredo Pareto (1848–1923) was the son of a French mother and an Italian nobleman. Having earned an undergraduate degree in mathematics and physics and then a degree in engineering from the Polytechnic Institute in Turin, Italy, Pareto first pursued a career as a consulting engineer to a railroad company and then moved to Florence as a director of a large iron works company.

Defeated in the Italian parliamentary elections of 1881 after running as a free trader and supporter of laissez-faire economics, Pareto later wrote numerous and scathing journalistic articles against Italian political, cultural, and economic backwardness and in favour of the free trade, laissez-faire principles of classical economic liberalism. As well, during this period, Pareto began producing a series of articles in classical liberal economics that were to earn his appointment to the Chair of Political Economy at the University of Lausanne in Switzerland in 1893.

At Lausanne, Pareto's initial primary focus was to develop economics into a pure, natural science. This he attempted to do by combining his abiding engineering interests in the mathematics and physics of systems in dynamic equilibrium with the classical liberal economic assumption of purely instrumentally "rational man," or what Weber referred to as *Zweckrational* man. In this vein, Pareto made numerous, indeed founding, contributions to the development of bourgeois mathematical economics, based on the assumption that all individuals within the economy act individually to maximize their returns while minimizing their costs.

At the same time, Pareto inaugurated a course in sociology at the University of Lausanne and began producing a series of sociological studies that, over time, came to dominate his interests, especially after 1898 when he inherited a large fortune from his uncle. By the time he had retired to a villa on the shores of Lake Geneva in Switzerland in

1909, he had abandoned his belief in a "pure" economics based on purely instrumental rationality in favour of developing a "pure" natural science of sociology based on the virtual omnipresence of human irrationality.

For Pareto, sociological analysis, like pure economics, had to be rooted in nothing other than strictly natural scientific, instrumentalist logic if it were to be rational and objective. Every other form of analysis would, he asserted, be "non-logical"—that is, non-rational or irrational. Thus, Pareto limited the logic or rationality of social scientific inquiry to instrumentalist logic only (Weber's *Zweckrational*-ity) in which the goals of action are already known or assumed and logic is merely the efficient maximization of effective means to the preconceived goal.

In Pareto's argument, then, value-directed rationality (Weber's *Vertrational*-ity) in social science became, by the magic of definition, non-logical, and not rational. The ideological usefulness of this definitional sleight of hand, reducing all rational knowledge and science to instrumental efficiency considerations only, was immediately evident in one of his earliest sociological works, *The Socialist Systems* (1901). In this work, Pareto attacked all forms of socialism, including Marxist-inspired socialism, for their "humanitarianism" and, therefore, their deeply non-logical or non-instrumentalist roots. Humanitarianism, Pareto demonstrated to his abundant self-satisfaction, could not be strictly instrumentalist because it repeatedly raised questions of value and of ends. And if it was not instrumentalist, it was, by *his* definition, non-logical.

Vilfredo Pareto's social theory stands out among all other classical sociological theories for its vigorously anti-humanitarian, anti-Enlightened value-stance, given its reduction of all rationality to merely instrumentalist considerations. Whereas the Enlightenment thinkers had viewed science as a means to achieve the end of human emancipation, Pareto reduced science to being an abstract means to discover better means to preconceived ends.

Pareto's anti-Enlightened despising of humanitarianism in social scientific theory is matched, in his sociological works, only by his anti-Enlightened rejection of the potential of the vast majority of humanity. In his earliest sociological writing, Pareto had determined that the vast majority of social thinking and social action was fundamentally non-logical or non-instrumental and was ruled by instinctual, irrational *sentiments* to which humanitarian appeals were but one, particularly vapid, expression.

Having begun his academic work as a classical liberal economist who helped mathematize and systematize economics as the study of individually maximized "utility" through the purely instrumental, "logical" behaviour of "rational man," Pareto had come to the not very insightful realization (except that it still remains beyond the comprehension of most mainstream economists) that a great deal of human behaviour, even in the marketplace, was not, in reality, instrumental-rational. But, unlike Max Weber, for instance, who theorized the growing domination of instrumental rationality in meaningful social action, Pareto's social theory attempted to make non-rational behaviour the overwhelming consideration in sociology. Indeed, Pareto attempted to found a natural science of sociology with human irrationality as its unchanging, necessary, and eternal cornerstone.

In his lengthy and amazingly unrigorous and opaque theoretical work, *Treatise on General Sociology* (1916), Pareto presented his basic argument that an array of unchanging and irrational sentiments causally controls everyday human reasoning, choices, and actions, as well as the justifications for such reasoning, choices, and actions. In this theory, everyday reasoning, choices, and actions are reduced, by definitional fiat, to being merely *residues* of the underlying irrational and unchanging sentiments. All justifications for reasoning, choosing, and acting are defined as merely *derivations* from the underlying and determining irrational sentiments.

In his theoretical practice, Pareto regularly conflated bedrock sentiments with residues, arguing that residues were the empirical manifestation of sentiments. Sentiments, which Pareto most often claimed to be biologically inherited "instincts" or irrational impulses, were thereby conflated into sociocultural behaviour and beliefs. Nowhere did Pareto actually investigate in detail the relative rationality, or even the relative instrumentalist rationality, of particular instances of everyday reasoning, choosing, and acting. Rather, his typical approach was to choose examples that he then would assert could be nothing but residues of irrational and unchanging sentiments since they were "obviously" impulsive or, alternatively, did not efficiently and effectively connect to the stated goal.

In his *Treatise on General Sociology*, Pareto listed six classes of residues that supposedly expressed the underlying sentiments: 1) the "instinct for combinations"; 2) the "instinct for group persistence" or "persistence of aggregates"; 3) the "need of expressing sentiments by external acts"; 4) "residues connected with sociality"; 5) the "integrity of the individual and his appurtenances"; and 6) "the sex residue." Of these six classes of residues, the first two were of paramount importance in Pareto's actual analyses.

The first class of residues, the instinct for combinations, was said to be the basic, instinctual foundation of the "ability to think," of "inventiveness," of "ingenuity," and so on. Thus, all reasoning, both logical and non-logical, was rooted in an imputed biological instinct. The presence of more of this instinct in some people than in others was said to

propel such a biologically favoured few to become inventors, specula-
tors, politicians, and the like.

The second class of residues, the instinct for group persistence,
explained, for Pareto, the enduring nature of kinship groups, ethnic
groups, and of social classes, for instance. For Pareto, this second, "con-
serving" class of residues was often "naturally" in opposition to the first
class of residues, which were change-oriented. Class 2 residues were said
to have a much greater distribution among the masses of humanity
than the Class 1 residues, which characterized the few.

The relative over-distribution of Class 2 residues accounted, according to Pareto, for the normal predominance of "good subordinates" in
the mass of society. The relative under-distribution of Class 1 residues
accounted, according to Pareto, for the natural predominance of the
"elite" few over the essentially conservative many. Thus, Pareto theorized a world of humanity in which the vast majority was, by its very
instinctual/sentimental nature, more conservative and more subordinate than the dynamic elite few. Pareto had thus found a "natural" or
"scientific" means to assert his anti-humanitarian value-stance.

Pareto also proposed four classes of derivations, or "non-logico-
experimental theories," by means of which all humans sought to
explain and justify what they thought they were thinking, choosing,
and acting upon by appealing, ultimately, to the underlying eternally
unchanging sentiments. These four classes of derivations were: 1)
"assertions," most commonly associated with Class 1 residues; 2)
appeals to "authority," which are most commonly associated with Class
2 residues; 3) "accords with sentiments or principles," which can be
related to all the classes of residues; and 4) "verbal proofs" through
sheer rhetoric, which can also be related to all classes of residues.

While Pareto regularly claimed to be applying a rigorous natural scientific logic to the sociology of sentiments, residues, and derivations,
his "general sociology" can readily be viewed as an exemplar of non-
logico-experimental derivations in practice. What counted for Pareto,
in his actual theoretical practice, was his steadfastly anti-rational, anti-
Enlightened value-stance.

For Pareto, society was a *system in equilibrium*. Equilibrium was maintained by the force of unchanging and eternal sentiments. These
sentiments ensured a regular return to balance of the social system.
Fundamental and supposedly observable uniformities in human nature
and behaviour, determined by bedrock sentiments, also ensured fundamental and observable uniformities in social organization.

While both the external appearances of social organization and the
various justificatory derivations for the shape of any given society were
continually changing, the overwhelming presence of irrational sentiments in social life would ensure a regular return of society to a

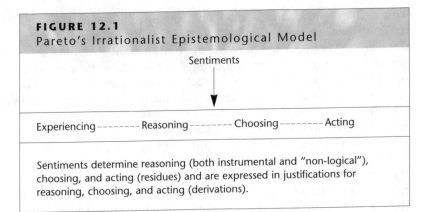

FIGURE 12.1
Pareto's Irrationalist Epistemological Model

Sentiments

Experiencing - - - - - - - - Reasoning - - - - - - - - Choosing - - - - - - - - Acting

Sentiments determine reasoning (both instrumental and "non-logical"), choosing, and acting (residues) and are expressed in justifications for reasoning, choosing, and acting (derivations).

balanced state of dynamic equilibrium between sentimental forces. This equilibrium was dynamic because it was said to be "undulatory," ebbing around the unchanging and eternal irrational sentiments.

The task of the pure sociologist was to determine, as "unsentimentally" and as instrumentally rationally as possible, the *social utility* of a given society, the degree to which the parts constituting the society efficiently and effectively served the existing state of affairs. The pure sociologist was to accept the existing state of societal organization as the given goal of all its constituent units. With this acceptance of the societal status quo as the "good" (+), the pure sociologist's task was merely to assess the efficiency and effectiveness of the parts within the system to the maintenance of that system.

For Vilfredo Pareto, transformative social change was clearly not possible (–). The unchanging and eternal sentiments necessarily reassert themselves through their control over human nature and, thereby, constitute strict limits to the degree of undulation that was "naturally" allowable within social organization.

Much of Pareto's theory of non-radical, undulatory social change was inspired by Niccolo Machiavelli's (1469–1527) much earlier instrumentalist and unsentimental analysis of the means by which governing power could efficiently and effectively beget more power. As well, Pareto borrowed from his contemporaries. From Georges Sorel (1847–1922) he learned the importance of political leadership's appeals to the irrational in the sentiments of the "masses." From Gaetano Mosca (1858–1941), he took, without giving credit, the notion of the "circulation of governing elites."

In *The Rise and Fall of the Elites* (1901), Pareto reduced what he called "class circulation" to the *circulation of elites* within a ruling class. In this work Pareto distinguishes between two kinds of people: the *elite* few, who are born with higher abilities and who acquire better skills, and the "non-elite" or mass of society. Within the elite few, Pareto further distinguished between the *governing elite* and the non-governing elite. The elite few were typically distinguishable from the masses by their much greater "capacity" and the usual predominance of Class 1, as opposed to Class 2, residues. The governing elite was distinguished from the non-governing elite by its willingness to use force when it appeared to be necessary to control the masses.

Pareto conceived of the vast majority of humanity as biologically and socioculturally unfit and unable to govern their own lives, let alone the life of the state. Because the masses, inevitably, were mindlessly ruled by irrational sentiments, they forever would need the direction of the few who, by fluke of the distribution of sentiments, as well as by breeding, were both fit and willing to govern. Thus, by definition, the majority of humanity was incapable of self-rule, and social change could never produce the conscious self-emancipation of humanity.

What appeared to be sociopolitical change was, for Pareto, most often only the renewal of the governing elite in order to maintain its rule over the vast majority by sustaining a proper balance or dynamic equilibrium between Class 1 and Class 2 residues within the elite. Specifically, there had to be a proper balance between foxes, who had plenty of Class 1, and ruled through "craft," "fraud," and "deceit," and lions, who had plenty of Class 2, and ruled by "courage," "fervour," and frequent resort to force.

Despite Pareto's continual claims to scientific objectivity, *The Rise and Fall of the Elites* was almost entirely devoted to advising the governing elite on how to engineer their continued rule efficiently and effectively. In that work, for instance, Pareto advised the elite on how to keep renewing a balance of Class 1 and Class 2 residues by co-opting the "best" of the essentially mindless mass into the ranks of the elite. As well, he advised them on how to appeal to the masses primarily on the bases of their irrational sentiments, and not on the bases of logic, which the masses were eternally incapable of comprehending. But most important, Pareto advised the elite never to hesitate in the use of force as soon as it is seen to be needed; "if the masses are not whipped when they are bad, then they will only grow wilder."

Failure to follow his instrumentalist advice on the efficient and effective social engineering of continued elite rule could end up in "revolutions," as Pareto made clear near the end of his *Treatise on General Sociology*:

> Revolutions come about through accumulations in the higher strata of society—either because of a slowing-down in class circulation, or from other causes—of decadent elements no longer possessing the residues

TABLE 12.1
Pareto's Stance on Humans, Existing Societal Organization, and the Possibility of Radical Social Change

Human potential	The vast majority of humanity is irrational, ruled by sentiments (High −)
Existing societal organization	In a state of dynamic equilibrium necessarily governed by an elite in continual flux (High +)
Possibility of radical social change	Impossible, only elite circulation possible (High −)

suitable for keeping them in power, and shrinking from the use of force; while meantime in the lower strata of society elements of superior quality are coming to the fore, possessing residues suitable for exercising the functions of government and willing enough to use force.

When they did occur, such revolutions could be only strictly political revolutions, not transformative social revolutions. The "elements of superior quality" from "the lower strata" would inevitably become the governing elite over the necessarily and eternally irrational majority. Radical *social* change was impossible (−) for all time and in every place.

In a later work, *The Transformation of Democracy* (1921), Pareto argued that the elite had also to maintain a balanced equilibrium between too much and too little centralization. In a case study of Italy, in which it was argued that too much decentralization of power had eroded efficient and effective rule over the majority, Pareto continued developing his view of "democracy" as elite rule by, primarily, subterfuge and a frequent overemphasis of Class 1 residues. Sooner or later, he predicted, the equilibrating pendulum would have to swing back towards rule by outright force and an overemphasis on Class 2 residues. Overly decentralized democracy by deceit, which refused to use force against the masses, would necessarily yield to centralized rule by force, when combined with an equally necessary shift in the economic pendulum from good times to hard times.

In this way, Vilfredo Pareto predicted and justified as necessary what was to become fascist rule in his own country and elsewhere. Indeed, Benito Mussolini (1883–1945) claimed to be much influenced by

Pareto's social theory. For his part, Pareto praised early fascism's vitality and resort to force. Perhaps, more than any other single contribution, Pareto's social theory had provided Mussolini with the theoretical justification for his regular claim that "fascism had no theory"; fascism, Mussolini claimed, was merely a concerted expression of the sentiments of the people.

Key Sources

Parts of *The Socialist Systems* have been translated from the French in S.E. Finer's edition of *Vilfredo Pareto: Sociological Writings* (Frederick A. Praeger, 1966). An abridged and, therefore, somewhat more readable version of Pareto's *Treatise on General Sociology* is in Elizabeth Abbott's edition of *Compendium of General Sociology* (University of Minnesota Press, 1980). Pareto's elite engineering theory is best captured in his *The Rise and Fall of the Elites* (Arno Press, 1979) and *The Transformation of Democracy* (Transaction Books, 1984).

Useful reviews of the context of Pareto's work and its impact include: J.H. Meisel's edition of *Pareto and Mosca* (Prentice-Hall, 1965); A. James Gregor, *Italian Fascism and Developmental Dictatorship* (Princeton University Press, 1979); and Richard Bellamy, *Modern Italian Social Theory: Ideology and Politics from Pareto to the Present* (Stanford University Press, 1987).

Some Suggestions for Research and Debate

1. Discuss Pareto's reduction of scientific logic to instrumentalism. To what degree is this reduction accurate in the working logic of natural science and of social science?
2. Is there a middle road between an Enlightened stress on human reasoning and Pareto's anti-Enlightened stress on sentiments? If not, why not? If so, is that middle road available to only a few or to all?
3. Discuss Pareto's theory of sentiments, residues, and derivations as an appeal to "common sense" that serves the interests of continuing rule by an elite.
4. Discuss Pareto's theory of the circulation of elites as an appeal to "common sense" that serves the interests of continuing rule by an elite.
5. Is rule by an elite inevitable or is transformative change possible?

Emancipation II:
Vladimir Lenin's Theory
of Uneven Development,
Imperialism, and Socialist
Revolution

THIRTEEN

Vladimir Ilich Ulyanov (1870–1924), who later assumed the surname
Lenin, was born into a comfortable family in Simbirsk, Russia. His
father, who had risen to the post of a provincial inspector of schools,
died when Lenin was only fifteen years of age; slightly more than a year
later, his elder brother was executed for attempting to assassinate Tsar
Alexander III. Active in illegal anti-tsarist activities throughout his education, Lenin graduated at the top of his class in law at St Petersburg
University in 1892.

Lenin's adult life was dedicated to the revolutionary transformation
of the conditions of exploitation and extreme oppression that characterized tsarist Russia. He has, of course, become most famous for his
political leadership of the Russian Revolution of 1917. As such, both his
admirers and detractors have recognized him to be a brilliant political
practitioner, able to grasp the potential of a given situation and turn it
to the advantage of the side that he was fighting for.

On the other hand, Lenin's social theory has often been discounted
for being unorthodox or inconsistent with Marx's Marxism. Instead of
following the orthodox Marxist approach of developing historical-
materialist theory on the basis of careful analysis of the forces and relations
of production, using that theory to guide practice, and then refining
the theory based on the lessons derived from a critical review of that
practice, Lenin is claimed to have merely and opportunistically altered
his theory, helter-skelter, to justify whatever practices were seen to be
required at the given moment.

Nothing could be further from the truth, or so we will argue. Indeed,
as the major theorist of the world's first socialist revolution, Lenin
made numerous and vital contributions to Marx's emancipatory social
theory. These core theoretical contributions are of such high quality
that they deserve to be carefully read and critically evaluated both on

their own merits and as crucial advances to Marx's Marxism. After such careful assessment, the serious student of social theory can determine the degree to which Lenin's own practices in the period of retrenchment and survival in the face of capitalist onslaughts and the failure of other revolutions in Europe (1919–24) were actually inconsistent with his core theorization from the late 1890s to 1918. Like the abuses, theoretical and practical, of Marx's Marxism by many others calling themselves Marxists, the vital core of Lenin's Marxism-Leninism is not to be confused with the many later so-called Marxist-Leninists who, in the name of Marxism-Leninism, regularly ignored or actively debased Lenin's (and Marx's) core social theory.

In the first instance, Lenin's ability to grasp the political potential within a given social situation was profoundly rooted in his classically Marxist theoretical analysis of the phases of the historical development of the forces and relations of production in Russia. His first major work, *The Development of Capitalism in Russia* (1899) was written in direct opposition to the varieties of Russian populists who claimed that capitalism was an unnatural or foreign implantation upon the soil of "natural" Russian communalism and was therefore doomed to organic failure. In this work, Lenin creatively and insightfully applied Marx's theorization, in *Capital*, of the phases of the historical development of capitalism within Britain in order to analyse in detail the emergent phases or "natural history" of a much less advanced, but nevertheless profoundly indigenous, capitalism in Russia.

After having consulted and digested more than five hundred statistical reports and books on the topic, Lenin argued that capitalism in Russia had developed indigenously, though relatively slowly and unevenly, throughout the Russian countryside and from there had invaded the cities. On the basis of first "usury" and then "merchant capital," much of the peasantry had been "freed" from its land base in order to work first in low-technology "manufactories" in the towns and then, increasingly, within the factories of "industrial capitalism" in the cities. Yet, capitalism remained chained and held back by the social organization of tsarist autocracy. The bourgeois political and economic revolution remained to be accomplished in order then to provide the conditions for socialism.

The Development of Capitalism in Russia is an exemplar of the detailed Marxist analysis of *uneven capitalist development*. It provides a rigorous analysis of local and societal conditions for the development of the forces and relations of production. Indeed, this volume is one of the earliest instances of the systematic and critical use of census data in social analysis and has, or should have, a methodological importance in social science akin to Durkheim's *Suicide*. Most important for our purposes, Lenin's first major work actively contributed to the theoretical development of Marxism as such.

Like Marx, Lenin linked each phase in the development of the forces of production to phases in the development of specific class relations. Lenin also creatively linked the development of specific class relations to the development of "stages" of emancipatory consciousness that were available within the different material situations of a highly variegated "peasantry," "semi-proletariat," and "proletariat," on the one hand, and an indigenous "bourgeoisie" on the other. For Lenin, the level of class consciousness was always related to the level of capitalist development in which the worker toiled and against which she or he struggled.

Most specifically, Lenin argued that, because of the directness of its exploitation and the collective concentration of its socialization in large-scale industry, the industrial proletariat was, within the context of its emergent struggles, the most capable of all the exploited and oppressed classes and class segments of becoming conscious of the class bases for exploitation. Because of the relative indirectness of their exploitation, their dispersal in the process of production, and the very immensity of the sociocultural oppression that they faced day-to-day, the peasantry and semi-proletariat were much less capable, from within their own experiences, of attaining a thoroughgoing class consciousness in struggles against their oppression.

Besides the greater conscious revolutionary potential of the Russian industrial proletariat, Lenin argued, this group's actual historical origins within the exploited and immensely oppressed peasantry and semi-proletariat, made it the "natural" *vanguard* of all the exploited and oppressed in the struggle against tsarism and for democracy. The Early Marx had explained the proletariat's centrality to emancipation on the basis of its being the most oppressed and alienated segment of society. Lenin applied the insights of the Later Marx to develop, in detail, a more Marxist argument for why the uneven development of capitalism had itself created a class that was capable of consciously expressing the democratic interests of the even more oppressed in civil society—a class that was actually capable of consciously leading itself and the rest of the oppressed against tsarist autocracy and for democracy.

As *The Development of Capitalism in Russia* made clear, the Russian bourgeoisie remained tied to its historical roots in the oppression and exploitation of all of the rest of society, including the rural peasantry and semi-proletariat. The bourgeoisie was, therefore, the "natural" ally of the landlords and tsarist reaction. Tied as it was to the oppression of the vast rural majority, such a bourgeoisie would never introduce the kind of democracy that could enable the entire countryside to develop towards advanced capitalism and democracy, and thereby create the conditions for a transformation to socialism.

Thus, for Lenin, despite its small size, only the industrial proletariat could consciously lead itself and the rest of the exploited and oppressed in Russia in the direction of "radical democracy" and, thence, socialism. From the turn of the century until the First World War, Lenin was chiefly concerned with addressing the conditions within which the vanguard, democratic revolutionary capacity of the industrial proletariat would actually be advanced.

In the innocuously titled *Strike Statistics in Russia* (1910–11), Lenin masterfully analysed the mass of official government statistics that became available after the huge wave of strikes in Russia during the 1905–06 period. This analysis demonstrated that the best-organized workers in the largest industrial plants had been first off the job, followed by the other workers. These, the "most advanced workers," had also been the most enduring, the most audacious, and the most tenacious in pressing their political demands. They were, in historical fact, followed by the other workers who, inspired by the leadership of the advanced wing of the industrial proletariat, turned their strictly economic demands to more widely political demands.

Thus, *Strike Statistics in Russia* demonstrated the vanguard role of the industrial proletariat, and in particular its most advanced wing, in collective class struggles. It demonstrated that "strictly economic" or "trade union consciousness," which was concerned only with bettering the situation at one's immediate workplace, could and would, through the experience of massive strikes, develop into "political consciousness," which made demands on the state.

The big question was how political consciousness could be further developed into "social democratic" or *socialist consciousness*, which sought the radical transformation of the existing autocratic state through a revolutionary struggle led by the working class and its industrial proletariat vanguard. On the basis of his findings concerning the uneven development of capitalism in Russia, the different levels of working-class consciousness that were likely to develop in the actual day-to-day practices of this variegated working class, and the vanguard role of the industrial proletariat, Lenin theorized and developed his practical answer to this big question: through a *revolutionary party "of a new kind."*

For Lenin, the development of socialist consciousness required not only the everyday conditions for trade union consciousness and the particular, pre-revolutionary conditions of crisis that would facilitate political consciousness. In order for trade union and political consciousness to develop into socialist consciousness, the correct intervention and concerted leadership of a revolutionary party that was guided by creatively applied Marxist theory was, in historical-material reality, necessary. Thus, as summarized in Figure 13.1, Lenin's epistemology

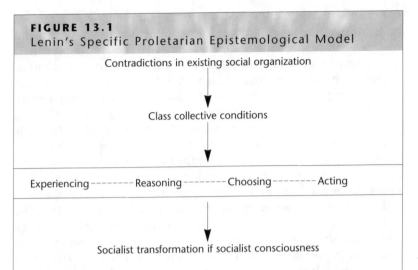

FIGURE 13.1
Lenin's Specific Proletarian Epistemological Model

Contradictions in existing social organization

↓

Class collective conditions

↓

Experiencing ――――― Reasoning ――――― Choosing ――――― Acting

↓

Socialist transformation if socialist consciousness

3 Types of consciousness

Strictly economic or trade union consciousness (reasoning, choosing, and acting) is derived from experiencing the forces and relations of production at the immediate workplace. The industrial proletariat is most likely to attain this level.

Political consciousness is derived from experiencing massive strike and protest actions especially in pre-revolutionary periods. Usually led by the industrial proletariat.

Socialist consciousness is derived from the above only if combined with the revolutionary party's correct intervention and concerted leadership in workplace and political struggles guided by Marxist theory and practice.

included a differentiation in types of consciousness, each of which was linked to the experience of different social conditions.

Such a revolutionary party of a new kind would have to be capable of facilitating and guiding the self-emancipation of the entire working class and poor peasantry in relatively "backward" Russia through the period of the democratic and then the socialist revolutions. It would have to do so by raising the consciousness of, first, the most advanced workers, and, then, other workers and poor peasants, to socialist consciousness through its organized "agitation" and "propaganda." Among other matters, such a party would have to be firmly rooted in the most advanced sectors of the working class, in all areas of working-class and poor peasant livelihood, as well as in all anti-autocratic social movements. It would, in other words, have to be capable both of expressing and of advancing the goals of the most advanced sectors of the proletarian vanguard to the rest of the working class and poor peasantry and also to the rest of society. This party would have to be sufficiently well-organized across Russia in order to facilitate the attainment of the conscious and collective self-emancipation of the working class. Equally important, it would have to know and struggle against the class-rooted positions of all other contending political factions in order to demonstrate the real necessity and possibility of a radically anti-tsarist, democratic revolution in Russia and the proletariat's necessarily leading role within it.

Using his theory of the uneven development of capitalism in Russia as the basis for his confidence in the revolutionary spirit of the working class and poor peasantry, Lenin argued, from 1905 onward, that the party must emerge from its underground form of organization. This underground form had been originally proposed by Lenin in *What Is to Be Done? Burning Questions of Our Movement* (1902) in order to fulfil the task of assaulting the autocracy. The party could now discard its secretive and purely professional structure in favour of an open organizational form that would attract new working-class members, especially young workers, in their "hundreds and thousands" into a party that was both democratic and centralized.

This organizational concept, *democratic centralism*, was clearly presented in a series of articles written in 1905 and 1906. Under the "democratic" aspect, current party members were called upon to apply the following principles of party organization: "to work tirelessly to make the local organizations the principal organizational units of the Party, in fact and not merely in name, and to see to it that all higher-standing bodies are elected, accountable, and subject to recall." The centralism aspect included "universal and full *freedom to criticize*, so long as this does not disturb the unity *of a definite action*." In other words, party members should freely debate but, once a decision has been arrived at, should act in concert to attain jointly decided policies by jointly decided means.

By the First World War and the break-up of the Second Socialist International due to the unprincipled support for war by almost all the social democratic parties in the contending countries (but not by the Russian party), the nature of capitalist development had, in the social theory of many Marxists, clearly changed from being competitive and progressive to being monopolistic and degenerate. In another of his major works, *Imperialism, the Highest Stage of Capitalism* (1916), Lenin argued that *imperialism*, the latest and "final" stage of capitalism, had five principal features.

> (1) The concentration of production and capital has developed to such a high stage that it has created monopolies which play a decisive role in economic life; (2) the merging of bank capital with industrial capital and the creation, on the basis of this "finance capital," of a financial oligarchy;

(3) the export of capital as distinguished from the export of commodities acquires exceptional importance; (4) the formation of international monopolist capitalist associations which share the world among themselves; and (5) the territorial division of the whole world among the biggest capitalist powers is completed.

From these five historical-material features, many of which had also been advanced by other Marxists and even by some non-Marxists of the time, Lenin drew a number of revolutionary implications that set him apart.

For Lenin, the monopolistic features of imperialism not only demonstrated capitalism's decadence and the necessity of socialism; the monopolistic organization of capital on a world scale also provided the real, material bases for socialist revolutions and national liberation movements on a world scale. The socialist revolutions would likely begin in the "weakest links" within global capitalist domination, such as in Russia, and not in the major imperialist centres, where a significant minority of the working class had been pacified by being granted shares in the fruits of imperialist domination. The ongoing imperialist war (the First World War) only heightened the contradictions within monopoly capitalism and further facilitated the global advance to socialism.

Under the conditions of actually existing imperialism, Lenin argued that the Russian working class and its party was faced with the crucial task of making a *socialist revolution* that would spark revolution in the rest of the world, particularly the rest of Europe. Under the new conditions of imperialism, the Russian working class and its party could not stop at merely attaining capitalist democracy. The party had to lead the way to socialism by seizing state power by and for the working class. The success of socialist revolutions in Europe would, in return, provide the material conditions for Russia to solve the massively real problems of its non-democratic past.

So confident was Lenin in his historical-materialist analysis of contemporary imperialism and in the growing revolutionary consciousness and action of the Russian working class and poor peasantry that he produced, in the months immediately before and immediately following the October Revolution, his definitive theorization of the principal social content of the new revolutionary socialist state in the process of being created in Russia through creative class struggle. This theorization is contained in *The State and Revolution* (1917) and in a whole series of articles leading up to that work and immediately following it.

In these works, Lenin argued that the appropriate general form of socialist organization had been incontrovertibly demonstrated by Marx in his account of the Paris Commune. The worker-controlled, self-emancipating "commune-state" was, in other words, the appropriate

105

formal substance of the socialist state. Secondly, Lenin argued that the Russian working class and soldiery had spontaneously discovered the commune form and had given it a concrete content in their self-organization into *soviets* during the struggle to get rid of the tsar. The soviets, then, were the concrete content of the commune form of working-class self-government and self-emancipation. Lastly, Lenin argued that the economic and administrative mechanisms that imperialism had produced in order to dominate the world had also made feasible, for the first time in human history, the democratic integration of public state activities into the whole of society by means of the commune or soviet state.

The new soviet/commune socialist state was to be profoundly democratic:

> Democracy must be *built* at once, from below, through the initiative of the masses themselves, through their effective participation in *all* fields of state activity without "supervision" from above, without the bureaucracy.... Democracy from below, democracy without an officialdom, without a police, without a standing army; voluntary social duty guaranteed by a *militia* formed from a universally armed people—this is a guarantee of freedom which no tsars, no swashbuckling generals and no capitalists can take away.

The central objective of *The State and Revolution* and of many other articles immediately preceding the revolution was to show why this soviet/commune, socialist democracy was both necessary and feasible *immediately* in Russia. Historical-material or "objective" conditions made socialist state organization immediately necessary. Imperialism or "state-monopoly capitalism" had so systematized and simplified the organizational world that real socialism had become objectively feasible. The advances in working-class consciousness in a revolutionary situation provided the principal "subjective" conditions for both the necessity and feasibility for immediate soviet/commune socialism.

By March 1918, Lenin had made it clear on numerous occasions following the October victory that the soviet/commune socialist state was to be rooted in the same organizational principle on which the revolutionary party of a new kind had been rooted eighteen years previously—democratic centralism. As a principle of state organization, democratic centralism combined a stress on democracy, as discussed above, with centralized, *worker-led* state agencies that were accountable to the grassroots organizations. In this way, Lenin argued, both Marx's profoundly democratic Paris Commune aspect and the aspect of "dictatorship of the proletariat" over the bourgeoisie and its allies could and would be assured.

TABLE 13.1
Lenin's Stance on Humans, Existing Societal Organization, and the Possibility of Radical Social Change

Human potential	Highly positive view of consciousness, especially among the proletariat and other exploited and oppressed classes (High +)
Existing societal organization	Highly negative—productive forces and social relations are in contradiction and intolerable, especially under imperialism (High –)
Possibility of radical social change	Socialist emancipation possible through revolutionary class struggle led by the proletariat and its party (High +)

"Socialism cannot be implemented by a minority, by the Party. It can be implemented only by tens of millions when they have learned to do it themselves." From "The Tasks of the Proletariat in the Present Revolution" (April 1917), through *The State and Revolution*, to the original version of "The Immediate Tasks of the Soviet Government" (March 1918), this had been the basic argument, consistent with Lenin's social theory as it had developed from 1899 onward. By the conclusion of the final draft of "The Immediate Tasks of Soviet Government" (April 1918), however, Lenin was arguing in favour of a "special stage of the socialist revolution," a period of "manoeuvring and retreating" forced upon the Russian Revolution by objective and subjective circumstances.

An extraordinarily difficult, complex and dangerous situation in international affairs; the necessity of manoeuvring and retreating; a period of waiting for new outbreaks of the revolution which is maturing in the West at a painfully slow pace; within the country a period of slow construction and ruthless "tightening-up," of prolonged and persistent struggle waged by stern, proletarian discipline against the menacing elements of bourgeois laxity and anarchy—these in brief are the distinguishing features of the special stage of the socialist revolution in which we are now living.

Provided that this "special stage of the socialist revolution" is clearly distinguished from Marx's and Lenin's actual social theory of socialism, the recognition of the necessity of a "special period" of something-much-less-than-socialism is not necessarily antithetical to Lenin's (or Marx's) core social theory. On the other hand, any glorification of many of the specifics of "manoeuvring and retreating" during the period of the special stage—for instance, the reduction of the meaning of socialism to not much more than state ownership of the major means of production, the re-creation and bureaucratization of a highly coercive state apparatus, and the absolute dominance of the party and party leadership over working-class self-activity—as being integral to Marxist-Leninist social theory flies in the face of that theory. Such glorifications directly contradict Lenin's own critical and self-critical understanding of that special stage.

Key Sources

Vladimir Lenin's writings are all contained in the forty-five volumes of his *Collected Works* (Progress Books, 1960–70). *The Development of Capitalism in Russia* is in volume 1; his early writings on democratic centralism are in volume 10; *Social Statistics in Russia* is in volume 16; *Imperialism the Highest Stage of Capitalism* is in volume 22; the relevant writings during 1917 and 1918, including *The State and Revolution* are in volumes 24–26.

The best overview of Lenin's social theory is Neil Harding, *Lenin's Political Thought: Theory and Practice in the Democratic and Socialist Revolutions* (Humanities Press, 1983).

Suggestions for Research and Debate

1. To what degree does Lenin's theory of the uneven development of capitalism apply in your country?
2. Have there been periods when at least some of the working class in your country has had political consciousness? If yes, how so and why? If no, how not and why not?
3. Have there been periods when at least some of the working class in your country has had socialist consciousness? If yes, how so and why? If no, how not and why not?
4. Has imperialism, as Lenin defined it, vanished in the world today? Or has it been altered? Or is it substantially the same?

Emancipation III:
Rosa Luxemburg's
Dialectical Materialism
and the Critiques of
European Marxisms

FOURTEEN

Rosa Luxemburg (1871–1919) was born in Zamosc in the southeastern part of Poland, which was then under the control of Russian tsarism. She grew up in Warsaw under comfortable circumstances within an Enlightened Jewish family whose principal source of living was her father's ownership of a timber business. Already active in underground revolutionary activity during her high-school years in Poland, Luxemburg fled into exile in 1889, joining other exiled Marxists in Switzerland.

Having first studied mathematics and natural science, she graduated, in 1897, from the University of Zurich with a doctorate in political science. During her university studies, Luxemburg had kept in close contact with events in Poland, co-founding first the Polish Socialist Party in 1892 and then, two years later, a more revolutionary Social Democratic Party when the earlier group rapidly embraced bourgeois nationalism as its main banner. After her studies, she eventually settled in Germany and very quickly became a leading theorist and spokesperson for the left-wing of the German Social Democratic Party, at the time Europe's largest socialist party and the most prestigious "Marxist" party in the world.

From her doctoral dissertation on, Rosa Luxemburg always tried to interrelate internationally and to assess critically the crucial economic and social developments in Poland, Russia, and Germany in the light of world capitalist development and working-class struggle. As an internationalist and a revolutionary, her abiding central question was: How and why was socialism both necessary and possible?

With this central question continuously in mind, Luxemburg in her theoretical work wove together analyses of both the immediate necessity and immediate possibility of working class–led emancipatory socialism. For her, both the immediate necessity for and possibility of

FIGURE 14.1
Luxemburg's Proletarian-Emancipatory Epistemological
Model

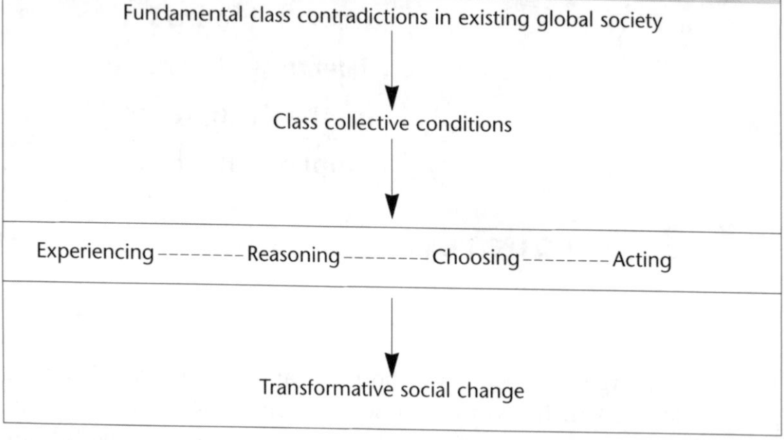

Fundamental class contradictions in existing global society

Class collective conditions

Experiencing ------- Reasoning ------- Choosing ------- Acting

Transformative social change

socialism arose from the specificities of global capitalist development and class struggles. In this sense, her epistemology, as indicated in Figure 14.1, recalls that of Marx. Rosenberg believed that vigorous critiques of socialist organizations and leaders who, she argued, were misleading the socialist movement on the question of immediate socialist transformation were requisite. By the time of her murder in 1919 by paramilitary thugs sent to capture her by the very German Social Democratic Party that she had tried so hard to transform, she was viewed by even those that she had most vigorously attacked as certainly one of the greatest Marxist theorists since Marx.

The core of Luxemburg's theoretical approach in her critiques of both capitalism and of socialist theories and organizational alternatives was her general method of *dialectical materialism*. Inspired by her complete agreement with Marx's basic value-stance (human potential +, existing societal organization –, radical transformation +), as indicated in Table 14.1, Luxemburg advanced Marx's general dialectical and materialist methodology by emphasizing the importance of grasping and interrelating the *contradictory totality* of *social* reality (both the economic base and the political and cultural superstructure) as it conditions and is itself altered by social action. Identifying the central contradictions within the historically changing totality became her trademark approach in all her diverse and extensive analyses.

With *Reform or Revolution* (1900), Luxemburg early established herself as the first and foremost Marxist critic of "reformist" social theory within the German Social Democratic Party and the Second International.

TABLE 14.1
Luxemburg's Stance on Humans, Existing Societal Organization, and the Possibility of Radical Social Change

Human potential	Highly positive view of practical-critical activity, especially by the proletariat (High +)
Existing societal organization	Highly negative—global productive forces and social relations are in contradiction and intolerable (High –)
Possibility of radical social change	Immediately possible through massive class struggle by the proletariat (High +)

111

The immediate cause of her critique was the publication of a series of articles by Eduard Bernstein in the party's theoretical journal, which was edited by Karl Kautsky. Bernstein, a major Social Democrat and one of the literary executors of Engels's estate, attempted to refute the central tenets of Marxism or what was called, following Engels, "scientific socialism." Among other matters, Bernstein argued that capitalism could, theoretically, *evolve* into socialism since the contradictions within capitalism were disappearing; thus, a radical class struggle was neither necessary nor fruitful. Social evolution, not revolution, was therefore the order of the day. The gradual additive impact of guided social reforms was, Bernstein argued, both necessary and sufficient to ensure the humanizing of capitalism and its slow withering away into socialism.

In response Luxemburg argued that:

> The scientific basis of socialism rests, as is well known, on three principal results of capitalist development. First, on the growing anarchy of capitalist economy, leading inevitably to its ruin. Second, on the progressive socialization of the process of production, which creates the germs of the future social order. And third, on the increased organization and consciousness of the proletarian class, which constitutes the active factor in the coming revolution. Bernstein pulls away the first of the three fundamental supports of scientific socialism. He says that capitalist development does not lead to a general economic crisis.
>
> ... But then the Question arises: Why and how, in that case, shall we attain the final goal?... If one admits with Bernstein that capitalist development does not move in the direction of its own ruin, then socialism ceases to be objectively necessary.

Without a focus on the internal contradictions of the capitalist totality, Bernstein's guided reforms intended to advance the socialization of labour and his gradualist program for the increased organization and consciousness of the working class become merely "means of adaptation" to capitalist exploitation and oppression and "Utopian," "idealist" wishful thinking.

Certainly, Luxemburg argued, the struggle for democratic reforms was one crucial side of the totality of the struggle to create socialism. But, it was only one side of the totality of social reality. Without the other side, the objective necessity of transformation, reforms could not be evaluated and prioritized based on their contribution to strengthening the organization and consciousness of the proletariat for its self-emancipation. One-sided reformism was, for Luxemburg, not only anti-Marxist and idealist; in our terms, it also necessarily tended towards becoming only another form of elitist social engineering in which an elite of "socialist" leaders guided the essentially mindless mass towards a better society through gradual social reforms that ensconced the leadership within the capitalist state. Thus, "Bernstein's book is of great importance to the German and the international labour movement. It is the first attempt to give a theoretic base to the opportunist currents common in the social democracy."

Luxemburg's two-sided, dialectical materialist approach and her revolutionary internationalist value-stance facilitated her critique of reformism in Germany and within the Second International. Her rigorous approach was also the central basis for her critique of what she saw to be deviation from scientific socialism in Lenin's social theory as it was developing in the context of the struggle against tsarism in Russia.

In *What Is to Be Done? Burning Questions of Our Movement* (1902) and elsewhere prior to 1905, Lenin had argued two major positions based on his analysis of the real situation of tsarist repression and the viciousness of the attack on the organized working class in Russia at the time:

1. The real experiences of the proletariat made it virtually impossible for it to develop, by itself and through its immediate struggles, a sufficiently socialist consciousness that would guide it to the transformation of capitalism. Only a party of "professional revolutionaries" steeled in Marxism and drawn, by necessity, primarily out of the ranks of intellectuals, could bring to the proletariat "from without" a socialist consciousness.
2. The immediate situation called for a highly centralized, top-down form of party organization in order to survive the tsarist onslaught until the working class was massively in motion again.

In "Organizational Questions of Russian Social Democracy" (1904), Luxemburg responded to the second of Lenin's major points by critiquing what she saw to be the organizational "ultracentralism" of Lenin's *What Is to Be Done?* To her, Lenin's formation of an "all-powerful" central committee of "conspirators," who would direct the revolution from above and outside, threatened the third basic tenet of scientific socialism, the self-emancipation of the working class.

> The only "subject" which merits today the role of the director is the collective "ego" of the working class. The working class demands the right to make its mistakes and learn in the dialectic of history.
>
> Let us speak plainly. Historically, the errors committed by a truly revolutionary movement are infinitely more fruitful than the infallibility of the cleverest Central Committee.

From 1905 on, Lenin was to incorporate much of Luxemburg's critique of ultracentralism in his development of the concept of democratic centralism.

Luxemburg's *The Mass Strike, the Political Party, and the Trade Unions* (1906) attempted, like Lenin had done, to draw lessons from the massive uprising of workers in Russia during 1905 in order both to critique Lenin's first point about the necessity of socialist consciousness coming to the working class "from without" and, at the same time, to attack the quiescence and lack of militancy of German Social Democracy. In this work, Luxemburg was the first to point out the importance of the worker-controlled soviets that had been spontaneously created in the heat of the mass strike. To her, as for Lenin, the mass strike and the soviets were clear evidence of the ability of the working class to attain, through its own experience of class struggle, a political consciousness of itself. German Social Democracy's hesitance to endorse the mass strike as a crucial, working class–led means of struggle demonstrated once again, its gradualist and controlling tendencies.

For Luxemburg, the mass strike and, in general, spontaneously emerging forms of class struggle *could* be sufficient for the establishment of socialism. In contrast, Lenin consistently argued that socialist consciousness, in so far as it required the ability to see capitalism and the struggle for socialism clearly, in its totality (in relation to all classes and movements, and in the light of Marxism), *and* without bourgeois ideological blinders, required the revolutionary party's intercession. In our terms, then, Luxemburg conceived of the party's primary task with respect to the working class as clarifying the basic choices that needed to be made in order to attain self-emancipation. Lenin, however, argued that the party had to intervene in both the reasoning and choosing of the working class in order to create the subjective conditions for working-class self-emancipation. Nonetheless, both agreed with Marx on the ultimate goal.

To the degree that Lenin's position of socialist consciousness "from without" included Marx's own principle of continually learning from the actual conditions and struggles of the working class and then returning the theorized results to the working class, his position against Luxemburg's endorsement of "spontaneity" seems to be the more dialectical materialist of the two. Yet Luxemburg's overstated advocacy of working-class revolutionary spontaneity did, at the very least, warn against any form of elitist social engineering "from above," be it reformist or "socialist," that would rob the working class of its self-emancipation.

Throughout her intellectual and political life, Luxemburg frequently argued with Lenin over their differing perspectives on what has been called the *national question*. Luxemburg contended that in most areas of the world, such as Poland, national self-determination had ceased to be a "progressive" bourgeois issue and had indeed often become the banner of reactionary forces, bourgeois or otherwise. Thus, for her, Lenin's espousal of the general right of national self-determination was a dangerous pandering to reactionary forces and not revolutionary at all. While Lenin came to qualify his general support of national self-determination with a concrete analysis of the specific circumstances for actually supporting the right in practice, Luxemburg never really altered her general opposition to national rights of self-determination.

Luxemburg's *The Accumulation of Capital* (1913) was her major application of dialectical materialism to the analysis of the historical changes in capitalism and its central contradictions since Marx's time. In that work, she argued that Marx, by restricting his analysis of the "realization" of capital (in volume 2 of *Capital*) to only relations internal to the capitalist mode of production as such, had insufficiently theorized the totality of capitalist development. Instead, Luxemburg contended, in order for capital to continue to be accumulated it had to be realized (commodities had to be sold and profits earned) through the incorporation and destruction of "non-capitalist modes of production" and living. In other words, in order to continue, capitalist exploitation had to incorporate, forcibly whenever necessary, all other non-capitalist areas of the world.

As capitalist development continued to incorporate and destroy non-capitalist modes of production, it, according to Luxemburg, increasingly approached the absolute limit of its existence, with no other non-capitalist areas to incorporate. As it approached its absolute limit, the contradictions within capitalism would necessarily become exacerbated and violent, and the situation of the vast majority of workers and near-workers would become increasingly desperate. Thus, what Luxemburg called *barbarism*, the forced destruction of everything not capitalist, was a fundamental and growing feature of contemporary capitalism. Barbarism was not principally a feature of early capitalist development, as Marx had argued in his analysis of primary or "primitive accumulation" in volume 1 of *Capital*. Continually expanding barbarism was, for Luxemburg, necessary to continued capitalist development.

By herself ignoring the unevenness of internal capitalist development as such and thus its "internal" ways of extending its existence, Luxemburg was able to define *imperialism* as simply "the political expression of the accumulation of capital in its competitive struggle for what remains of the non-capitalist environment." *Militarism*, therefore, becomes increasingly vital to capitalism, both as a means to forcibly incorporate the "other" parts of the globe and maintain supremacy within the existing capitalist states *and* as itself an increasingly profitable "province of accumulation."

> Capitalism is the first mode of economy with the weapon of propaganda, a mode which tends to engulf the entire globe and stamp out all other economies, tolerating no rival at its side. Yet at the same time it is also the first mode of economy which is unable to exist by itself, which needs other economic systems as a medium and soil. Although it strives to become universal, and, indeed, on account of this its tendency, it must break down—because it is immanently incapable of becoming a universal form of production, in its living history it is a contradiction in itself, and its movement of accumulation provides a solution to the conflict and aggravates it at the same time. At a certain stage of development there will be no other way out than the application of socialist principles. The aim of socialism is not accumulation but the satisfaction of toiling humanity's wants by developing the productive forces of the entire globe. And so we find that socialism is by its very nature a harmonious and universal system of economy.

Socialism or barbarism had increasingly become the only available choice, between which there was no middle ground. However, even as the necessary war approached, the increasingly "opportunistic" leaders of German Social Democracy were searching for "peace utopias." Karl Kautsky, then held to be the leading Marxist theorist in Europe, had even written about how and why global peace might be possible under capitalism. To Luxemburg, instead of leading the workers and their allies towards socialist transformation, the leaders of German Social Democracy were stupefying them with impossible dreams.

On 4 August 1914, the entire legislative caucus of the German Social Democratic Party voted to provide funds for the kaiser's war effort. To Luxemburg, this was the single most disgraceful and opportunist event in the history of the socialist movement. This deed went directly against the Social Democratic Party's own stated internationalist principles and program; it also trashed the stated policy of the Second International calling upon all workers to immediately strike against the war—a policy drafted by Luxemburg and Lenin in 1907 and often reiterated in the formal agreements of the German party.

The Crisis in German Social Democracy (1916, also known as *The Junius Pamphlet*) was Luxemburg's analytical and practical response. In this pamphlet she vigorously assaulted the leadership for its absolute opportunism, blamed the failure of most social democratic parties in western Europe on their failure to uphold scientific socialism, lauded the revolutionary and internationalist socialism of the Russian party under Lenin, and prepared a number of theses for the formation of a new, actually socialist party.

In jail for her anti-war and pro-socialist agitation, Luxemburg composed a first draft of her initial evaluation of the Russian Revolution of 1917 (published without revision as *The Russian Revolution* in 1922). In this draft, her expressed intention was to explain both the "fundamental significance" of the Russian Revolution and its material, organizational, and programmatic limitations or errors to the German working class. She believed that once the German working class was aware of both the significance and the necessary limitations of the Russian Revolution, the class, despite its misleadership by Social Democracy, would do everything in its power to transform Germany into a socialist society and thus raise itself up from its ignominious participation in the First World War and fulfil its internationalist duty.

For Luxemburg, the fundamental significance of the Russian Revolution was that the Bolsheviks, led by Lenin, had "dared" to seize political power and to *begin* the revolutionary process of collectively creating a socialist globe. They had done so despite the tremendous economic-social-cultural difficulties in "backward" Russia during a losing war.

> This is the essential and enduring in Bolshevik policy. In this sense theirs is the immortal historical service of having marched at the head of the international proletariat with the conquest of political power and the practical placing of the problem of the realization of socialism, and of having advanced mightily the settlement of the score between capital and labour in the entire world. In Russia the problem [of the realization of socialism] could only be posed. It could not be solved in Russia. And in this sense, the future everywhere belongs to "bolshevism."

Because it was the first and because it occurred in a "backward" country facing tremendous problems, the limitations and errors of the first socialist revolution were, to her, fully understandable, although never to be glorified. Such errors and limitations would, she was certain, be rectified in the context of socialism being created throughout the rest of Europe under much better economic-social-cultural circumstances in countries with long democratic traditions.

Shortly after co-founding the Communist Party of Germany, Rosa Luxemberg was murdered. In "Notes of a Publicist" (1922), Lenin—the comrade she had worked with so closely and debated so critically—wrote: "Not only will Communists all over the world cherish her memory, but her biography and her *complete* works ... will serve as useful manuals for training many generations of Communists all over the world." As simply an exemplar of emancipatory social theory, Rosa Luxemburg's dialectical materialism can also be similarly recommended.

Key Sources

The two principal sources of Rosa Luxemburg's works referred to in this brief chapter are Mary-Alice Waters's edition of *Rosa Luxemburg Speaks* (Pathfinder Press, 1970) and Luxemburg's own *The Accumulation of Capital* (Routledge and Kegan Paul, 1951). Further relevant writings are included in Horace B. Davis's edition of *The National Question: Selected Writings by Rosa Luxemburg* (Monthly Review Press, 1976).

Lenin's *What Is to Be Done? Burning Questions of Our Movement* is in volume 5 and his "Notes of a Publicist" is in volume 33 of his *Collected Works* (Progress Books, 1960–70).

J.P. Nettl's two volumes of *Rosa Luxemburg* (Oxford University Press, 1966) is a good, though entirely academic, source for Luxemburg's life and times. Lelio Basso, *Rosa Luxemburg: A Reappraisal* (Praeger, 1975), and Norman Geras, *The Legacy of Rosa Luxemburg* (NLB, 1976), provide more engaged scholarly accounts of her theoretical approach.

Suggestions for Research and Debate

1. Did Luxemburg's dialectical materialist theory sometimes lead her to be more dogmatic in her conclusions then Marx or Lenin? If not, why not? If so, why so?
2. Compare Luxemburg's view of imperialism to Lenin's. Which is more appropriate today? Why?
3. To what degree did Luxemburg's analysis of the Russian Revolution prove to be correct? In what ways did her analysis prove incorrect?
4. Given that one of her closest comrades, Clara Zetkin, was a leader of the women's movement in Germany, speculate on why Luxemburg was so silent, like almost all the men considered in this text, concerning the particular oppression and exploitation of women.

Emancipation IV:

Antonio Gramsci's Critique

of Economic Determinism

and Theory of Hegemony

and Intellectuals

FIFTEEN

Antonio Gramsci (1891–1937) was born in the agricultural village of Ales in Sardinia, Italy. The fourth son of a minor public official, Gramsci grew up in poverty and ill health. Awarded a scholarship to the University of Turin in 1911, he was forced to leave his studies in 1915 because of his health and impoverished circumstances.

From 1914 to 1919 Gramsci was a regular contributor to Socialist Party of Italy newspapers and a leading figure in the Turin branch of the party. During 1919 and 1920 he was a founding editor of *L'Ordine Nuovo* (*The New Order*), the main theoretical, educational, and mobilizing journal of the Turin factory council movement. In 1921 he became a central committee member of the newly formed Communist Party of Italy and eventually became its general secretary. He was arrested in November 1926 by Mussolini's fascist regime, and two years later was condemned to twenty years imprisonment. Shortly after being released from incarceration due to a series of severe illnesses, Antonio Gramsci died of a brain hemorrhage in April 1937.

Gramsci's path to historical materialism closely mapped his political activism. When Gramsci was an activist within the Socialist Party, his theoretical approach was thoroughly idealist, following the doyen of Italian cultural criticism, the philosopher Benedetto Croce. During his factory council days Gramsci developed Marx's (and Luxemburg's) analysis of the spontaneous potential of the working class to achieve its self-emancipation without the external guidance of a political party, comparing the factory councils to Lenin's theorization of the soviets as the new Paris Commune form. From 1921 until his incarceration, Gramsci worked tirelessly on building and reforming the Italian Communist Party upon the lines emanating from the Third International.

During the period of his incarceration, Gramsci finally took the time, in his *Prison Notebooks*, to attempt to advance historical materialism as

Marxist emancipatory social theory. This work, comprising thirty-two handwritten notebooks in all, is justly regarded as Gramsci's central theoretical contribution and is, therefore, what we will focus upon.

In the six volumes of the *Prison Notebooks* (much of which remains untranslated), the central question that held the fragments together, composed as they were under the duress of fascist imprisonment, was: Why has the socialist revolution failed to spread, so far, to advanced capitalism? In order to begin to answer this question from a solidly historical-materialist or Marxist perspective, Gramsci undertook a thorough critical rethinking of the idealism underpinning "spontaneity," on the one extreme, and economic determinism on the other. Gramsci thus critiqued the philosophic deficiencies of both his own former Crocean idealism and of the economic determinism in the version of Marxism that was often held to be Marx's Marxism within the international communist movement. He did so in order to re-establish Marxism and Marxism-Leninism as the *philosophy of praxis*, a theory that was capable of providing the working class with the resources required for self-emancipation under the conditions of advanced capitalism.

Recalling, and indeed rooted in, Marx's twin critiques of Hegel's idealism and of Feuerbach's vulgar materialism, Gramsci's critique of Croce's idealism and of the economic determinism of Nicolai Bukharin, a leading Russian "Marxist," was intended to "set Croce on his feet" instead of on his head. For Gramsci, Croce's idealism had performed the important philosophical task of critiquing a historical, "metaphysical" objectivity and determinism by reintroducing human consciousness and history into social-cultural analysis.

However, "The opposition between croceanism and the philosophy of praxis [Marxism] is to be found in the speculative character of croceanism." Croce's philosophical world is a world without human life, a world of pure concepts, a dialectic of the ideal "mind" and not of real "flesh and blood" humans. For Croce, it was not the concrete person who thinks, chooses, and acts, but the "spirit" that thinks itself through the person. Using a biological analogy, Gramsci argued that real humans did not inhabit Croce's world. "Croce's history presents 'boned' figures, lacking skeletal structure and possessed of flaccid, feeble flesh." This "flaccid, feeble flesh" or "superstructure" was, to Croce, purely spiritual/conceptual; in other words, real humans were "'boned' and devoid of a skeleton," or a material base for their consciousness, in Croce's idealism. The upshot was that historically creative, labouring human beings were replaced by idealist concepts and the elite that controls such conceptualizations: "history becomes a formal history, a history of concepts and in the final analysis, a history of intellectuals."

Whereas Croce's idealism was the philosophy of the deboned and not of human praxis, Bukharin's *Historical Materialism: A System of*

119

Sociology (1921) exemplified, for Antonio Gramsci, the other extreme—a vulgar materialist philosophy of a lifeless skeleton, the economic base, that was devoid of interaction with any living flesh, or superstructure. Bukharin's economic determinism and positivist, natural-scientific approach represented, Gramsci argued, a "degenerate" version of Marx's historical materialism in so far as it replicated the worst of Feuerbach's vulgar materialism that Marx, as we have seen, had so thoroughly criticized. The fact that Bukharin's approach had, in the main, become the catechetical version of Marx's Marxism was even more reason for Gramsci to root his own social theory in a return to the dialectic embedded in Marx's epistemology and actual historical materialism.

Like Marx's critique of Feuerbach, Gramsci attacked Bukharin's presentation of the "so-called orthodox tendency" of deterministic scientific socialism for merely substituting an abstract "material" conceptual certainty for the abstract certainty of the "idea." Marx's dialectic between the human subject as creator of history and the material objective conditions within which humans think, choose, and act was thereby replaced with the false certainty of "scientism."

The scientific socialism that Gramsci was in fact attacking was not the revolutionary social scientism of Rosa Luxemburg. Gramsci was attacking the particular approach that had been introduced, after Marx's death, in some of Frederick Engels's works, and had been further developed in the works of Karl Kautsky in Germany and G.V. Plekhanov in Russia. Its basic theoretical elements were positivism, dialectical naturalism, rigid *economic determinism*, and linear social evolutionism. Human knowledge of the real—meaning natural—world was seen by scientific socialists as "reflected," more or less, in human conceptualizations of that world, which were then posited in the natural scientific paradigm of cause and effect. Contradictions within the basic economic structure, or skeleton, completely determined the evolution of human history, including its moments of revolutionary development. Humans need only follow the guidance of the "truly Enlightened" in order to understand when and how capitalism would necessarily cease to be. In our terms, then, a "leftist" variant of elite social engineering theory had substituted itself for Marx's social theory.

For Gramsci, Marx's historical materialism provided the crucial dialectical advance on both categorical idealism and the ahistorical vulgar materialism of so-called scientific socialism. Marxism, for Gramsci (as for Marx), was a tendential, probabilistic, not nomothetic, social science capable of unifying the flesh and bone of real, human practical activity in the world, of integrating theory and practice, of analysing the dialectical relationship between the economic base and superstructure, and of assessing both the necessity and practical possibility of working-class self-emancipation. While it promised the absolute cer-

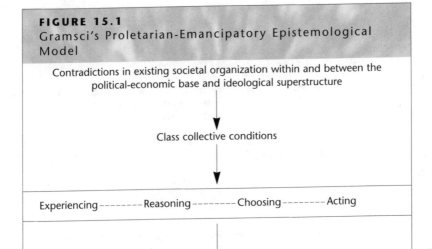

FIGURE 15.1
Gramsci's Proletarian-Emancipatory Epistemological Model

Contradictions in existing societal organization within and between the political-economic base and ideological superstructure

↓

Class collective conditions

↓

Experiencing --------Reasoning --------Choosing --------Acting

↓

Socialist transformation if counter-hegemonic

3 Types of hegemonic consciousness

Traditional (dominated by pre-bourgeois intellectuals)
Organic (dominated by bourgeois intellectuals)
Counter-hegemonic (requires revolutionary Marxist-Leninist party)

tainty of revolutionary transformation "in the fullness of time," scientistic socialism was actually, for Gramsci, anti-Marxist at its very core.

In its place, Gramsci recommended a return to both the epistemological roots and the value-stance of the socialist science of historical materialism. But, as illustrated in Figure 15.1 and Table 15.1, both Gramsci's epistemology and his basic value-stance were more clearly rooted in the historical dialectic between base and superstructure, between determinism and voluntarism, between theory/science and emergent praxis.

Gramsci rooted his alternative, dialectical, and non-scientific reading of Marx in the very passages of Marx's writing that seemed, to the vulgar materialists, to capture Marx at his most economic determinist, Marx's *Preface to the Critique of Political Economy*. Gramsci focuses on Marx's interrelation of the economic base and the superstructure, in which the forces and relations of production condition ideology, or the superstructure, such that humankind only sets for itself such tasks as it can resolve and a social order does not perish until the forces of production have reached their limits within the old order. Gramsci argued against the "degenerate," economic determinist interpretation of sub-

TABLE 15.1 Gramsci's Stance on Humans, Existing Societal Organization, and the Possibility of Radical Social Change	
Human potential	Highly positive view of practical-critical activity, especially by the proletariat and its intellectuals (High +)
Existing societal organization	Highly negative—productive forces and social relations are in contradiction and are in dialectical/contradictory relation to the ideological superstructure (High −)
Possibility of radical social change	Possible through class struggle by the proletariat if led by a counter-hegemonic revolutionary party capable of fighting both the war of position and the war of manoeuvre (High +)

sequent "Marxists" that saw only one form of consciousness (for each class) being derived from the given economic base of forces and relations of production. Instead, Gramsci argued that Marx had presented a *total*, dialectical model of capitalist society in which the economic base and the superstructure were interrelated such that in the final analysis the economic base determined a specific *range* of possible forms of consciousness. For instance, Gramsci's classic discussion of *Fordism*, the recently introduced re-organization of major industrial workplaces into assembly-line production under strict managerial controls, emphasized both the economic and the superstructural domination of the working class at work. Under Fordism, capitalists usurp both economic and cultural surplus value from the working class.

For Gramsci, the recognition of a range of consciousness being determined by the economic base was Lenin's most important theoretical advance within historical materialism. It was Lenin, after all, who had theorized why socialist/revolutionary consciousness was highly unlikely, no matter how necessary and appropriate it was with respect to the economic base, to spring directly from workers' experiences of contradictions within the forces and relations of production. Given the political dominance of the bourgeoisie over the entire superstructure, other forms of consciousness more acceptable to, and accepting of, the bourgeoisie (such as trade union consciousness) were, for Lenin and

Gramsci, much more likely to dominate working-class thinking and action unless there was the concerted intervention of the revolutionary party and its intellectuals into political practice.

For Gramsci, then, Lenin had successfully theorized bourgeois *domination* or coercion in working-class consciousness and had successfully led a party forged to confront and transform the domination of the bourgeois state as well as to socialize the economy. In Gramsci's militaristic terminology, the Russian Revolution had destroyed bourgeois coercion or domination through a *war of manoeuvre* or *war of movement*, a rapid frontal assault on bourgeois state domination.

While, to Gramsci, a war of manoeuvre was both necessary and probably sufficient in societies such as Russia with a very weakly developed bourgeois superstructure, it was necessary but not sufficient in advanced capitalist societies. The working classes in advanced capitalism had generally failed to follow the lead of the Russian Revolution, despite the fact that the basic economic conditions for socialism were much deeper and more widely spread than in Russia. They had generally failed precisely because the superstructure of advanced capitalism had developed in a way such that state coercion or domination in "political society" had been supplemented, and even occasionally superseded, by seemingly consensual, bourgeois "intellectual and moral leadership" within *civil society*, or everyday life. This intellectual and moral leadership within civil society Gramsci called *hegemony*. The theorization of hegemony was his crucial contribution to historical materialism.

In advanced capitalism, where bourgeois ideology was highly institutionalized in both political and civil society and was widely internalized, a relatively extended period of counter-hegemonic "trench warfare," a *war of position* within civil society, was necessary prior to the frontal assault or war of manoeuvre. A concerted and effective critique of bourgeois intellectual and moral leadership was required so that bourgeois hegemony would not be left standing after the frontal assault had "destroyed the outer perimeter" of capitalist domination. Without this war of position, "at the moment of their advance and attack the assailants would find themselves confronted by ... [an inner] line of defence which was still effective."

Constructing, maintaining, and renewing the inner line of defence within the civil society of bourgeois hegemony was, Gramsci argued, the chief task of bourgeois intellectuals. He defined intellectuals broadly as all those who exercise directive or high-level technical capacities in society. Intellectuals, for Gramsci, included both *traditional intellectuals*, such as ministers and creative artists, and *organic intellectuals*, who are more directly involved in the reproduction of capitalist society, such as technicians and managers, social workers, civil servants, school teachers and university professors, and journalists and mass media personalities. Organic intellectuals were seen to be especially crucial to the embedding of bourgeois hegemony in *common sense* or, more accurately, in the common senses of the various classes.

For Gramsci, the main problem with most shared common sense was not really that it often tended to be "disjointed," "episodic," and uncritical in and of itself. In capitalism, as in all class societies, the main problem with common sense is that "subaltern" or "subordinate" classes, unlike dominant classes, do not under "normal" circumstances possess their own critically developed and institutionalized superstructure. If they did, after all, they would not be subaltern. Subaltern classes are normally subjected to the leading influence or hegemony of dominating classes through the embedding of bourgeois ideology in common sense. Through the creative labour of bourgeois intellectuals, capitalist ideology—the superstructural justification of capital accumulation through exploitation and oppression—becomes embedded in the common senses of subordinate classes and, therefore, a real force in their lives, appearing to be rooted in their own consent.

Intellectuals who rejected both traditional and organic roles could choose to become collectively engaged in the trench warfare or war of position of rigorous counter-hegemonic struggle. This collective, counter-hegemonic struggle, which, for Gramsci, was best waged within the Communist Party, necessarily entailed confronting the suppositions, theories, analyses, and other practices of bourgeois intellectuals. But, more than just contesting "the philosophy of the philosophers," counter-hegemonic intellectuals had to be so rooted in the working classes that they could also effectively critique bourgeois ideology within the common senses of subaltern classes. Only then could the inner defences of capitalist domination within both the dominant and subaltern classes be so weakened that self-emancipatory socialist revolution would be actually possible in advanced capitalism.

A philosophy of praxis cannot but present itself at the outset in a polemical and critical guise, as superseding the existing mode of thinking and existing concrete thought (the existing cultural world). First of all, therefore, it must be a criticism of "common sense," basing itself initially, however, on common sense in order to demonstate that "everyone" is a philosopher and that it is not a question of introducing from scratch a scientific form of thought into everyone's individual life, but of renovating and making "critical" an already existing activity. It must then be a criticism of the philosophy of the intellectuals out of which the history of philosophy developed and which, in so far as it is a phenomenon of individuals (in fact it develops essentially in the activity of single particularly gifted individuals), can be considered as marking the "high points" of progress made by common sense, or at least the common sense of the more educated strata of society but through them also of the people. Thus an introduction to the study of philosophy must expound in synthetic form the problems that have grown up in the process of the development of culture as a whole and which are only partially reflected in the history of philosophy. (Nevertheless it is the history of philosophy which, in the absence of a history of common sense, impossible to reconstruct for lack of documentary material, must remain the main source of reference.) The purpose of the synthesis must be to criticize the problems, to demonstrate their real value, if any, and the significance they have had as superseded links of an intellectual chain, and to determine what the new contemporary problems are and how old problems should now be analysed.

For Gramsci, the very process of countering bourgeois hegemony was also the process of developing a new self-emancipatory hegemony within the thinking, choosing, and acting of the working class. Like Marx, Gramsci recognized that "everyone is a philosopher," that everyone is a social theorist with at least some degree of interrelated understanding of her or his everyday experiences.

The philosophy of praxis, or Marxism, in its contestation of the war of position was, if you will, Gramsci's "cultural" contribution to Marx's, Lenin's, and Luxemburg's "political-economic" analyses. With Gramsci, then, Marxism became a more complete social theory by incorporating into historical materialism the concrete analysis of the forces and relations of the economic, political, *and* the cultural.

Key Sources

The principal source in English of Antonio Gramsci's writings while he was imprisoned is Quintin Hoare and Geoffrey Nowell Smith's edition of *Selections from the Prison Notebooks* (International Publishers, 1971).

Joseph V. Femia, *Gramsci's Political Thought: Hegemony, Consciousness, and the Revolutionary Process* (Oxford University Press, 1981) provides the best discussion of Gramsci's writings during his prison period. Christine Buci-Glucksmann, *Gramsci and the State* (Lawrence and Wishart, 1980) is also an important secondary source. A generally good biography of Gramsci's entire life is Giuseppe Fiori, *Antonio Gramsci: Life of a Revolutionary* (NLB, 1975).

Suggestions for Research and Debate

1. Does bourgeois hegemony operate in your own common sense? If not, why not? If so, how does it limit your thinking, choosing, and acting?

2. Discuss a mass media account of some recent, large demonstration in your part of the world. How does that account contain aspects of bourgeois domination and of bourgeois hegemony?

3. Develop and discuss an emancipatory, counter-hegemonic account of that same demonstration. To what degree are counter-hegemonic accounts facilitated by collective discussion?

4. Using Gramscian concepts, develop a critical analysis of a recent sporting or musical event that you have attended. To what degree are the economic, political, and cultural components of the event intertwined and in contradiction?

The Middle Road III: Karl Mannheim's Sociology of Knowledge, Intellectuals, and the Third Way

SIXTEEN

Karl Mannheim (1893–1947) was born into a bourgeois Jewish family in Budapest, Hungary. While enrolled at the University of Budapest, he studied for a year under Georg Simmel at the University of Berlin and also came into contact with Max Weber's "middle road" approach. During the First World War and his student years, Mannheim became active in two distinct sides of Hungarian intellectual life. As a member of the Social Scientific Society, a broadly social democratic attempt to introduce positivism and empiricism into Hungarian national culture, Mannheim encountered the natural-scientific model of social science. Following Max Weber's intellectual lead, he quickly came to reject both positivism and empiricism as "wooden" and unable to address the real questions of meaningful social action.

On the other side, Mannheim's active membership in the Free School for Studies of the Human Spirit, a grouping of idealist intellectuals committed to cultural-ethical renewal by resolving what they perceived to be a "crisis of culture" within modernity, was to have more lasting impact. Within this grouping, Mannheim encountered a number of idealist approaches to epistemology, most notably Georg Lukacs's attempt to "Hegelianize" Marxism by centring on the reification of all spiritual life inherent in capitalism.

Mannheim's life work can be roughly summarized as the social-theoretical attempt to find a middle road between "mindless" positivism and empiricism, on the one side, and totalizing idealist or materialist approaches on the other. Throughout his work, he was in search of what might be a more adequate social-scientific approach that would facilitate much-needed social reforms within the context of cultural/ethical reform and renewal.

Mannheim's academic career was twice interrupted by forced exile. Having been appointed, under Lukacs's authority, as a professor of philosophy at the University of Budapest during the brief flowering of the Hungarian Soviet Republic in 1919, Mannheim was forced by the successful counter-revolution to seek university employment in Germany in 1920. Again, in 1933, having attained the prestigious professorship of economics and sociology at the University of Frankfurt, Mannheim had to flee to England to escape Nazism. In England, he professed sociology at the London School of Economics until shortly before his death in 1947.

The major influence of Hegelian philosophical idealism was clearly evident in Mannheim's early hermeneutic/interpretive epistemological essays. In "On the Interpretation of *Weltanschauung*" (1921–22), for instance, Mannheim was concerned with theorizing how the "spirit of an age"—the general world-view or *Weltanschauung*—structures the culture of a society and how it can be known. Following Hegel, Mannheim argued that this spirit was expressed in and could be known through particular cultural products, and that the meaning of cultural products was expressed in and could be grasped through interpreting the world-view.

In "Historicism" (1924), Mannheim began to move away from this static, circular, philosophical theorization of *Weltanschauung* to a more historical perspective on the topic. There, Mannheim located historicism, the advocacy of the continuing evolution and realization of meaning through history, as itself a totalizing world-view that was in the process of historical development in opposition to the atomism and universalism of "rationalism."

With "The Problem of a Sociology of Knowledge" (1925) Mannheim broke with his Hegelian focus on *Weltanschauung* as a complete cultural totality by critiquing Georg Lukacs's "Hegelianized-Marxist" argument that only the proletariat could attain a total view of the true nature of society. For Mannheim, as opposed to Lukacs, there could be no straightforward and direct correspondence between classes and full knowledge.

Instead of the Marxist working hypothesis concerning the structurally determined interests of differing classes, Mannheim developed a notion of the "indirect 'committedness'" to particular world-views of certain social groups that "champion" differing world-views in competition with each other. These competing world-views are all necessarily partial, Mannheim argued, and are only indirectly linked to class and other social bases. Their articulation, systematization, and development are all dependent on "the social composition of the intellectual stratum corresponding to" each competing world-view.

In "The Ideological and the Sociological Interpretation of Intellectual Phenomena" (1926), Mannheim recognized that Karl Marx had founded the first *sociology of knowledge*, but he critiqued Marx's approach for being too one-sidedly materialist and simplistic, too "ideological." In place of ideological Marxism, Mannheim proposed a more detached "sociological" approach that would provide an interpretation of competing world-views from "without" by considering the broad social context in which they arise and develop and by "functionally" relating the ideas to the "social-material" sphere without privileging one world-view over another.

"Conservative Thought" (1927) applied his developing social theory of knowledge to the historical analysis of nineteenth-century German conservative-romantic thought. Mannheim argued that German romantic conservatism was not merely a reactionary world-view but was, in its context, oppositional and in competition with the abstract, progressivist rationalism associated with the rising bourgeoisie. Mannheim then rooted this conservatism in the classes and social strata that were being marginalized within expanding capitalism—the feudal lords, peasantry, and small bourgeoisie. Such conservative notions as reclaiming the family and a view of society as an evolving organism were analysed through the texts of their intellectual spokespersons— the "mercenary pamphleteers"—and related to the specific social-material situation of declining classes and strata.

In "The Problem of Generations" (1928), Mannheim's dissatisfaction with the Marxist emphasis on class was finally expressed by the intro- duction of social location as a more comprehensive and adequate concept than class alone. *Generations* were viewed as temporal social locations that muddied or mediated the impact of one's class location on one's social ideas. Such age-based social locations required the con- tinual renewal of world-views by intellectuals from all generations in order to become embedded in a new generation.

"Competition as a Cultural Phenomenon" (1929) argued that inter- group relations were inherently competitive in both the economic and social spheres; thus, *competition* was inherent in the cultural-ideational sphere as well. By universalizing competition, Mannheim justified his particular sociology of knowledge with its emphasis on extrinsic com- parisons between competing world-views mouthed by competitive groupings of intellectuals. Thus Mannheim's sociology of knowledge was in opposition to the Marxist type, which emphasized not only competition between classes but also co-operation within classes and between classes and allies in the construction and practice of an ade- quate, relatively comprehensive world-view.

Ideology and Utopia (1929, expanded in 1936) was the culmination of Mannheim's social theorization of knowledge. In this work, he argued that, in general, the competitive struggle between social groups over power and domination underpinned variations in world-views advanced by intellectual spokespersons for the competing groups. *Ideology* was delimited to the system of beliefs of dominant groups.

129

Such groups "are so interest bound to a situation that they are simply no longer able to see certain facts which would undermine their sense of domination." On the other hand, the *utopian mentality* was seen as a future- or change-oriented, as opposed to backward-looking, world-view and was the appropriate world-view of rising classes and other social locations that resented the domination of the ruling ideology. Mannheim's central argument was that "Different interpretations of the world for the most part correspond to the particular positions the various groups occupy in their struggle for power."

Ideology and Utopia thus freely incorporated Marx's twin insights that the social-material conditions of one's existence tend to determine one's social consciousness and that humans therefore organize collectively either to change or to maintain those conditions. Yet in this work Mannheim continued to "generalize" upon Marx's focus on class relationships by replacing it with a much broader focus on a variety of social-historical locations, any of which could serve to define a particular world-view. In this way, like Max Weber had done with his introduction of status and power in addition to class location, Mannheim effectively discarded what for Marx and Marxists was the central key to unlocking a critical understanding of knowledge, of societal organization, and of the possibility of radical social change.

Marx had focused on ideology as the entire superstructure of class rule and had also vigorously, even ruthlessly, critiqued its major spokespersons by uncovering the class interests underlying their particular espousals of the dominant ideology. Mannheim, on the other hand, replaced Marx's historical-materialist notion of ideology with an idealist and historicist focus on world-views or *Weltanschauungen* as cultural totalities. He thereby eschewed the "particular" critique of spokespersons in favour of merely interpreting differences between available world-views, be they "ideological" or "utopian."

In place of Marxism and class consciousness, therefore, Mannheim proposed a "total" and "general" interpretation of competing world-views that would go "beyond" Marxism's critique of ideology and have "the courage to subject not just the adversary's point of view but all points of view, including his own, to the ideological analysis." In this way, Mannheim rejected Marx's argument that the purpose of social theory or philosophy was not just to understand the world, no matter how critically or sceptically, but to change it.

Thus, on the face of it, Mannheim's middle road sociology of knowledge privileged scholarly, extrinsic interpretation of all competing perspectives over the advocacy of any particular class-rooted stance. This "relationism," he admitted, was necessarily silent on the relative truth content of any such perspectives or world-view. Mannheim also asserted, but never explained, that his situationally determined rela-

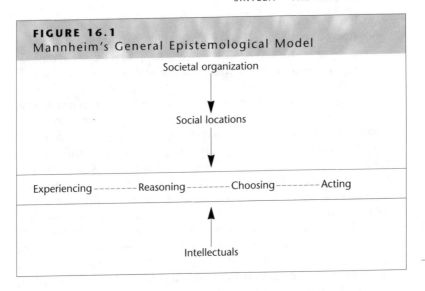

FIGURE 16.1
Mannheim's General Epistemological Model

Societal organization

Social locations

Experiencing -------- Reasoning -------- Choosing -------- Acting

Intellectuals

131

tionism did not fall into the irrationalist trap of "relativism," the argument that any particular view was "dependent upon the subjective standpoint and the social situation of the knower." On the question of "which social standpoint offers the best chance for reaching an optimum of truth," Mannheim was forced to remain silent within the context of his middle road social theorization.

As Mannheim made clear in *Ideology and Utopia* and even clearer in an essay written just before fleeing to England in 1933, published posthumously in *Essays on the Sociology of Culture* (1956), only one "stratum" of society had, in general, the potential to rise above its own social location and understand the perspectives of other social locations. This stratum, the *intellectuals* or *intelligentsia*, had the relatively unique "potential," he argued, to reach a broader, more comparative understanding of the world beyond its own particular roots.

In the first instance, intellectuals could rise above their particular social position because their position was relatively unique. The intelligentsia was, he argued, an "interstitial stratum" "between, but not above, the classes." Intellectuals, he argued, could be "socially unattached," unlike other strata such as workers and bosses. Secondly, because of their relatively extensive educational training and lifestyle of discussion and debate, intellectuals often had "to face the problems of the day in several perspectives," unlike other strata. For Mannheim, the intellectual:

> is *equipped* to envisage the problems of his time in more than a single perspective, although from case to case he may act as a partisan and align

himself with a class. His acquired equipment makes him potentially more labile than others. He can more easily change his point of view and he is less rigidly committed to one side of the contest, for he is capable of experiencing concomitantly several conflicting approaches to the same thing.

On the one hand, then, intellectuals such as natural scientists who were trained into only one perspective on truth—scientism—were presumably being robbed of their versatility and therefore their "general," inter-subjectively objective ability to comprehend the world. On the other hand, intellectuals who became "partisan" and took up the perspective of a particular class and/or party were reneging on their task as intellectuals to strive to remain as uncommitted and disinterested as possible, even if this meant being somewhat less grounded in reality.

Mannheim's sociology of knowledge was, thus, a direct assault both on positivism and empiricism, on the one side, and Marxism, on the other. His middle road social theory of knowledge directly entailed a conception of intellectual work as best being done, as much as possible, by being "labile" and multi-sided as opposed to being "partisan" and one-sided. As such, his middle road directly contradicted, for example, Antonio Gramsci's Marxist theoretical approach to knowledge and the importance of partisan intellectuals in the forging of a self-emancipating counter-hegemony. Mannheim, it seems, forgot that "labile" can mean both "flexible" and "unstable."

With respect to his own value-stance underlying his middle road sociology of knowledge, then, it should by now be apparent that Mannheim viewed human potential as being relatively restricted by one's social location, with the partial or potential exception of intellectuals. In other words, human potential was quite neutral (neither + nor –). Similarly, Mannheim's general view of existing societal organization was also generally neutral (neither + nor –): one's view of such organization was dependent upon one's social location within society, and it was the responsibility of authentic intellectuals to remain as neutral as possible under most circumstances. Lastly, on the question of the potential for radical social change, Mannheim's answer would appear to be a resounding "no" (–), since actually radical change would favour only one side of the competing world-views.

Upon fleeing Nazi Germany for England in 1933 and reflecting upon the tragedy of the contemporary human condition, Karl Mannheim dramatically altered the principal focus of his middle road social theorization. In both *Man and Society in an Age of Reconstruction* (1935, expanded in 1940) and *Diagnosis of Our Time: Wartime Essays of a Sociologist* (1943), for instance, Mannheim virtually abandoned the social theorization of knowledge in favour of the theorization and practical application of "democratic" social planning.

TABLE 16.1
Mannheim's Apparent Stance on Humans, Existing
Societal Organization, and the Possibility of Radical
Social Change

Human potential	Conditioned by social location except for intellectuals (Neutral)
Existing societal organization	Positive and negative views of societal organization are perspectival (Neutral)
Possibility of radical social change	Only guided reforms influenced by the stratum of relatively unattached and free thinking intellectuals are possible (–)

Such social planning, guided by newly committed intellectuals such as himself, had become absolutely essential, he argued. What Max Weber had analysed as rationalization had been advanced to such an extent by both liberal or laissez-faire capitalist rationalism and its Soviet state socialist variant that, as Weber had foreseen, the vast majority of individuals had turned over to an undemocratic elite minority "the responsibility of making decisions." Thus, there had appeared in both types of rationalist society a "growing distance between the elite and the masses."

These conditions of "mass society," as Weber had predicted, provided the principal basis for "the 'appeal to the [charismatic] leader' which has recently become so widespread" and for the more general glorification of "irrationality" in both thought and action. Thus, at that particular moment, it was incumbent upon middle-of-the-road intellectuals such as Mannheim to convince the existing elite in Western capitalist societies that it was in their best interests to create forms of support for, education of, and guided participation by the masses through democratic as opposed to "totalitarian" social planning.

Mannheim's self-styled middle-of-the-road approach to guided, elitist, yet somehow democratic, social reconstruction was, in historical fact, successfully advanced by many other middle-of-the-road intellectuals, such as John Maynard Keynes and John Kenneth Galbraith. Their intellectual leadership, together with the fear of both fascism and the mobilization of the working class for socialism, led to the postwar era of the welfare state, which was generally hegemonic in advanced capitalism until the 1970s.

Since then, of course, the rise of the neo-liberal assault on the welfare state, full employment, and the working class, aided by the apparent demise of the socialist threat to capitalism, has facilitated the resurrection to dominance of the old liberal laissez-faire ideology that had been theorized and popularized Herbert Spencer in the nineteenth century. Whether or not there can be a middle road between capitalism and socialism remains a moot point, to say the least.

Key Sources

The writings by Karl Mannheim that have been referred to in this chapter are found in: *Essays on the Sociology of Knowledge* (Routledge and Kegan Paul, 1952); *From Karl Mannheim* (Oxford University Press, 1971); *Ideology and Utopia* (Routledge and Kegan Paul, 1952); *Man and Society in an Age of Reconstruction* (Harcourt Brace Jovanovich, 1948); and *Diagnosis of Our Time: Wartime Essays of a Sociologist* (Routledge and Kegan Paul, 1943).

David Frisby, *The Alienated Mind: The Sociology of Knowledge in Germany, 1918–1933*, 2nd ed. (Routledge, 1992) sets the context for Mannheim's development of his sociology of knowledge. Brian Longhurst, *Karl Mannheim and the Contemporary Sociology of Knowledge* (St Martin's Press, 1989) provides both a solid overview of Mannheim's sociology of knowledge and a discussion of its impact on more recent theorizations.

Suggestions for Research and Debate

1. Compare (and contrast) Mannheim's sociology of knowledge to Marx's founding approach. Which is more insightful? Why?
2. To what degree was Mannheim's sociology of knowledge derivative of Max Weber's social theory? Explain your response in some detail.
3. Is Mannheim's sociology of knowledge actually relativistic? How so or why not?
4. Compare (and contrast) Mannheim's theorization of intellectuals to Gramsci's approach. Which is more insightful and why?
5. Was Mannheim's work on social planning consistent with his earlier social theorization of knowledge? How so or how not?
6. To what degree, if any, did Mannheim's approach to social planning differ from Emile Durkheim's elite engineering approach? Explain your response in some detail.

The Ongoing Relevance of Classical Theory for a Change: Vital Issues for Our Times and Your Theorizing

SEVENTEEN

From within the European tradition, classical social theory has, in varying ways and with differing intensities, centred upon the momentous changes in social organization that were introduced into human history with modernity, or the emergence and development of capitalism. Modernity originated in Europe and spread out from there to eventually encompass, if not enchain, the entire globe. Again, it is not too surprising that the classical social theorists of this change would have been Europeans. And given the profoundly imperialist, racist, and sexist manner in which capitalist class society transformed both Europe and the rest of the world during the nineteenth and twentieth centuries, it is not surprising that all of those who would have the luxury of extended social theorizing, or who would get to count as social theorists of these changes, would be white, and almost all would be male and from the ruling class or its allies.

What is more surprising, perhaps, is the real variation in theoretical approaches that did emerge, as we have seen, from the socially restricted purview of leading theorists, even in the heyday of European domination. In this text, my central concern has been to introduce the richness within the variety that did emerge, despite the obvious and not so obvious biases that each theorist carried into the profoundly social act of social theorizing.

The key additional concerns of this text have been: 1) to facilitate a comprehension of each theorist's key arguments by providing means of comparison among the theories considered; 2) to stress the necessity of reading the actual writings of these theorists, as opposed to remaining dependent on the summaries of others; 3) to provide a heuristic eureka-helper for the critical assessment of those readings; and 4) to urge the self-critical development of one's own social theorizing. Discussions of the basic epistemology and underlying value-stance of each theorist were

FIGURE 17.1
A Timeline of Classical Social Theory to the Second
World War

Elite engineering
Comte
(1798–1857)

    Spencer
    (1826–1903)

        Durkheim
        (1858–1917)
        Pareto
        (1848–1923)

Middle road

        Simmel
        (1858–1918)
          Weber
          (1864–1920)
            Mannheim
            (1893–1947)

Emancipation
    Marx
    (1818–83)

        Lenin
        (1870–1924)
        Luxemburg
        (1871–1919)
          Gramsci
          (1891–1937)

developed as a pedagogical device to help achieve these objectives while at the same time briefly developing each theorist's analysis of the development and impact of the social organization of capitalist modernity.

Overall, two major and antithetical value-stances with respect to human potential, societal organization, and the potential for radical social change have battled within the classical European tradition of theorizing modernity and its impact: the mainstream of elite engineering (– + –) and the radical counter-mainstream of emancipation (+ – +). In response to these two relatively consistent value-stances, another approach to the central problem of modernity within the European tradition has attempted to theorize a middle road between elite engineering and emancipation.

All three approaches were, in varying ways and differing intensities, themselves responses to the Enlightenment and the rise of capitalist modernity. This fact has enriched, as well as delimited, the problems addressed and the analyses produced in sociology. Without a serious examination and critical appreciation of the insights garnered by each of these approaches, current analyses of central issues will necessarily be less incisive and informed than they might have been and our practices will be less likely to lead to the results intended.

Figure 17.1 provides a summary timeline of theorists prior to the Second World War. Of course, the classical concerns of social theorizing did not die in the war. Since that time, a number of other important theorists have addressed the issue of the social organization of capitalist modernity and its implications for human development and social change in insightful and important ways. Almost all of these later theorists have documented, at least to a degree, their debts to the classical European tradition, even while attempting to vigorously critique all or significant aspects of that tradition.

Those who would purport to be introducing an entirely new approach to theorization, like some extreme postmodernists, can, I would assert, readily be seen to be carrying a great deal of baggage, wittingly or not, from particular value-stances that were first theorized within the classical European tradition. The tendency to assume away the impact of societal organization on social change and human potential, as if we could think away capitalist modernity, is entirely idealist and anti-historical, and not merely anti-structural. As well, we can now recognize, it is classically anti-sociological.

In my view, like capitalism itself, the classical European tradition and its main focus cannot be easily escaped in one's own social theorizing. The classical European tradition of social theory can be, and indeed must be, critiqued and then critiqued again for its frequent structured and unstructured silences with regards to sexism/patriarchy and to racism/imperialism. While, logically, these new approaches to social theory could incorporate value-stances different from those of the classical theorists, my own sense is that the most insightful contemporary approaches will continue to be developed within the ideological frameworks of what we have called elite engineering, the middle road, and emancipation.

Within the classics, the middle road, as we have seen, has floundered theoretically between the mainstream of elite engineering and the stormy seas of emancipation, often forsaking the middle route for a grudging recognition of the necessity for elite engineering. The emancipatory approach, while holding true to its basic value-stance in its theory, has also had a real tendency to sink in its practice into the mainstream of elite engineering. For its part, the mainstream continues to tack successfully between its liberal/neo-liberal and its paternalistic conservative appearances, developing the elite engineering approach in

137

onse to the issues raised and advanced, in the first instance, by the other two approaches. In all cases, there is plenty of theoretical work yet to be done.

In my own Marxist emancipatory view, the mainstream continues to dominate social theory because the class to which it is allied continues to rule *and* because neither of the other approaches has yet adequately theorized the full range of exploitation and oppression that capitalist modernity entails. The middle road has yet to theorize the real possibilities for the termination of global oppression and exploitation in capitalist modernity. Whether there actually is some effective middle road remains to be seen, but I doubt it. To a degree, the emancipatory approach has theorized the class basis of capitalism, from the perspective of human emancipation, but has failed, even now, to pursue a full theoretical analysis of working-class self-emancipation that recognizes women and non-whites as majorities within that class. Again, a great deal of work remains to be done.

Suggestions for Research and Debate

Comparing Approaches within the European Tradition
1. From within elite engineering, which theorist captures social reality most adequately? How and why?
2. From within the middle road, which theorist captures social reality most adequately? How and why?

The European Tradition as a Whole: Some Emphases and Silences
1. To what extent is the entire tradition aided by its rationalism? To what extent is it limited by it?
2. To what extent is the entire tradition aided by its Eurocentrism? To what extent is it limited by it?
3. To what extent is the entire tradition aided by its male-centredness? To what extent is it limited by it?

Linking the Classics to Current Theories
1. To what degree do contemporary feminist theories incorporate the value-stances and theoretical contents of classical European sociology?
2. To what degree do contemporary postmodernist theories incorporate the value-stances and theoretical contents of classical European sociology?
3. To what degree do contemporary social-psychological theories incorporate the value-stances and theoretical contents of classical European sociology?

Linking the Classics to Current Issues

1. Marx, Durkheim, and Weber are in the pub debating poverty in the world today. What are the key points that each makes? Who provides the best explanation? Why?
2. Marx, Durkheim, and Weber are in the pub debating nationalism in the world today. What are the key points that each makes? Who provides the best explanation? Why?
3. Marx, Durkheim, and Weber are in the pub debating malaise/ uneasiness in the world today. What are the key points that each makes? Who provides the best explanation? Why?

Critiquing the Surveyor

1. "The author of this text is biased by his value-stance." Identify his stance and show how that stance has both clarified and misinterpreted the writings of a social theorist considered in this text.
2. "The professor teaching this text is biased by his or her value-stance." Identify that stance and show how it has both clarified and misinterpreted the writings of a social theorist considered in this text.
3. "I am biased by my value-stance." Identify your stance and show how that stance has both clarified and misinterpreted the writings of a social theorist considered in this text.

Developing Your Theoretical Approach

1. What key concepts developed in the classics are vital for your own theorization of the social world? Why are they vital? How should they be further developed? What other concepts are key? Why?
2. What key interrelationships between concepts developed in the classics are vital for your own theorization of the social world? Why are they key? How should they be further developed? What other interrelationships are key? Why?
3. What key groupings and/or organizations analysed in the classics are vital for your own theorization of social change in the current world? Why are they vital? How should they be further developed? What other groupings and/or organizations are key? Why?